Myrna Whigham
Iowa State University
Curriculum and Instruction
N005 Lagomarcino Hall
Ames, IA 50011-3190

Emerging Trends in Teacher Preparation

This series is dedicated in loving memory
to my parents, Daisy Lea and Weldon F. Appelt.
Through their love and devotion for me, I learned to
believe in myself and what I might be able to achieve in life.

Emerging Trends in Teacher Preparation

*The Future
of Field
Experiences*

Editor
Gloria Appelt Slick

CORWIN PRESS, INC.
A Sage Publications Company
Thousand Oaks, California

For information address:

Corwin Press, Inc.
A Sage Publications Company
2455 Teller Road
Thousand Oaks, California 91320

SAGE Publications Ltd.
6 Bonhill Street
London EC2A 4PU
United Kingdom

SAGE Publications India Pvt. Ltd.
M-32 Market
Greater Kailash I
New Delhi 110 048 India

Printed in the United States of America

Library of Congress Cataloging-in-Publication Data

Emerging trends in teacher preparation: the future of field
  experiences / edited by Gloria Appelt Slick
      p. cm.
    Includes bibliographical references and index.
    ISBN 0-8039-6212-6 (alk. paper). — ISBN 0-8039-6213-4 (pbk.:
  alk. paper)
    1. Student teaching—United States.   2. Teachers—Training of—
  United States.   I. Slick, Gloria Appelt.
  LB2157.U5E44   1995
  370'.7'330973—dc20   95-7276

This book is printed on acid-free paper.

95 96 97 98 99 10 9 8 7 6 5 4 3 2 1

Corwin Project Editor: Susan McElroy

Contents

Foreword

Student teaching has long been considered the capstone of the teacher education program, and early field experiences have recently become a vital part of preparing teachers. Most teacher educators believe that field experiences should be integrated into the preparation of future teachers.

Because of this emphasis on field experiences, the position of director of field experiences has become even more important in teacher education. Where can field directors receive the information necessary to carry out the many and varied duties of the position? They tend to ask other field directors' advice. One of the most popular opportunities for field directors to share ideas is through membership in the National Field Directors' Forum, an affiliate with the Association of Teacher Educators.

The tenure of a field director is relatively short. The average tenure is between 3 and 5 years. Because of the turnover of field directors, there always seem to be new field directors literally craving information that will help them perform their duties.

Field directors recognize the need for some books that contain the information that both experienced and new field directors could use as a reference. A series of four books dealing with all aspects of field experiences, edited by Dr. Gloria Appelt Slick, fulfills the need. Directors around the nation welcome this series and I am proud to endorse this effort.

ELDEN R. BARRETT, PH.D.
FORMER PRESIDENT, NATIONAL FIELD DIRECTORS' FORUM

Foreword

Dear Educator:

As you read the material presented in this four-book series dealing with field experiences in teacher preparation programs, I hope you will bear in mind that this unique project is being brought to you from an institution whose history is rich in and founded upon teacher education. It has been through the leadership and dedication of such educators as Dr. Gloria Appelt Slick, editor of this series, that The University of Southern Mississippi, which was founded as Mississippi's normal school in 1910, continues to take a leadership role in the professional training of teachers.

I am proud to share with you this most recent endeavor of Dr. Slick, which focuses on the significance of field experiences in teacher preparation. Recent research by the Holmes Group, John Goodlad, and such accrediting agencies as the National Council for the Accreditation of Teacher Education has underscored the importance of the field experiences component of teacher education programs. This series of four books provides a review of state-of-the-art programs and practices in field experiences. The contributing authors represent prestigious teacher preparation programs from around the country. The information presented herein is solidly grounded in both research and practice. One of the main purposes of the four books is to provide practical guidelines for application of effective programs and practices in field experiences.

This is not the first time Dr. Slick has produced a national project that emphasizes field experiences. In 1993, through a national teleconference under the auspices of the Satellite Educational Resources Consortium, four interactive distance learning programs were broadcast to more than 200 sites nationally for the purpose of assisting student teachers, during their student teaching experiences, with their transition from university students to classroom teachers. From that series and the research involved to produce it evolved the current books, whose purpose reaches beyond student teachers and encompasses all persons, processes, and institutions affected by the field experiences component of teacher education. In both cases, Dr. Slick's overall goal has been to provide assistance and direction for all those involved in field experiences so that students of teacher education will be better prepared to meet the challenges of teaching the children of today and tomorrow.

Teacher education will always remain a major focus at The University of Southern Mississippi. We are committed to excellence in our teacher preparation programs and strive to develop the best of each of our students' abilities and expertise as future teachers. It is through such efforts as Dr. Slick's that we strive to meet that commitment.

Best wishes,

AUBREY K. LUCAS
PRESIDENT, THE UNIVERSITY OF SOUTHERN MISSISSIPPI

Preface

$\mathbf{A}$s a result of the Holmes Report, "A Nation at Risk," and other research, the wheels have been set in motion for a reflective and systemic change in the education profession. Both public schools and institutions of higher learning have had the national, public spotlight on the quality of their educational outcomes and teacher preparation programs, respectively. Institutions of higher learning have adjusted their content and pedagogical requirements in their teacher education programs to try to meet the challenges of children who are products of the information age. Public schools have updated curricular offerings and made concerted efforts to tackle the innumerable problems relative to providing students and faculties with safe environments in which to teach and learn. Research by such educational leaders as Goodlad, Berliner, and Boyer emphasizes that the teachers of the future will need to participate early and continuously during their teacher preparation programs in the public school arena where they will eventually be employed. Nationwide, school districts and universities are forming collaborations that not only provide insight into the culture of the teaching profession for the novice teacher but also offer opportunities for veteran teachers to retool their skills as well as share their expertise with upcoming generations of new teachers. In essence, this bridge between the universities and the public schools, whether in the form of a professional development school, or a lab school, or local public school campus, provides the pathway from student to teacher.

The program planning and management required to provide students in teacher preparation programs the opportunity to successfully cross the bridge from student to teacher are very complex. The bulk of the responsibility for providing students this successful crossing relies upon the collaborative success of teacher preparation programs and offices of educational field experiences. The director of the field experiences programs plays a principal role in managing the various persons and systems involved in the transitional passage of students to beginning teachers. It has been well documented by research that field experiences are the pivotal turning points in students' preparation for becoming teachers. During those experiences theory meets practice, and students discover whether they can teach—or even want to teach. To date, for all persons and entities involved in this process, there is very little, if any, material available to assist in providing the best possible experiences for students aspiring to become exemplary teachers. The goal of this series of books is to provide field directors the information and practical guidance necessary to design and implement a successful field experience program that will provide individuals in teacher preparation programs a smooth transition from student to teacher.

Because the focus of these books is to provide information and practical guidance to all persons involved with field experiences in teacher preparation programs, it became a foregone conclusion that those persons contributing to this book should either be currently affiliated or have been recently affiliated with field experience programs. Most of the authors have actually been field experience directors, with the exception of those in specialty areas such as law and public school administration. In order for the book to be representative of a national view of the issues related to field experiences, much time and effort went into selecting persons representing a variety of types of institutions as well as geographic locations around the country. Attention has been given to the size of the teacher preparation programs offered at the various institutions that are represented in the books, with the intent to provide as many relevant views about field experience programs as possible in order to benefit cohorts everywhere. Institutions represented from the southeast include the states of

Alabama, Louisiana, Mississippi, Florida, and North Carolina; the
northeast includes the states of New Jersey, New York, Pennsylvania, and Delaware; the midwestern states include Ohio, Kentucky,
Illinois, Michigan, Iowa, Indiana, and Minnesota; the central
states include Oklahoma and Texas; and the western states include
Colorado, Arizona, Utah, and California.

Organization of the Books

To provide information and practical guidance for all the
issues related to field experience programs, there are four books,
each with a specific purpose. Book I, *The Field Experience: Creating
Successful Programs for New Teachers*, provides information about
the development and organization of field experience programs.
It presents state-of-the-art field experience programs and explains
what kinds of experiences should be provided to students. Other
issues in Book I include the dilemma of the department chair who
must provide a program that creates a balance between theory and
practica, the dean's perspective of the significance of field experiences in teacher training, and the evaluation processes needed for
field experiences programs. Book II, *Preparing New Teachers: Operating Successful Field Experience Programs*, presents practical ideas
concerning the operation and function of the field experiences
office and takes into account state department requirements relative to certification that also have an impact on field experience
programs. Such issues as placement procedures as well as dis-
placement procedures and the legal ramifications of both are
discussed. The multifaceted responsibilities of the field director
are presented, which brings to light the public relations that the
director must handle, not only with the public schools but also
across the various colleges and departments at a university/
college. In addition, the purposes of field experiences handbooks
are explained. Book III, *Making the Difference for Teachers: The Field
Experience in Actual Practice*, addresses the needs and responsibilities of the persons involved in a typical field experience
paradigm—the university student, public school personnel, and
university personnel. Key issues like effective communication and

classroom management skills, effective mentoring, and adequate training of cooperating teachers are presented. Field experiences are explained from the student teacher's perspective, and the process of the student's assimilation of the culture of teaching is addressed. A major issue of concern is the preparation of cooperating teachers for the responsibility of supervising students. This is also dealt with in Book III. In addition, suggestions are made for ways to express appreciation to those who work so diligently supervising student teachers and other practicum students. Each of these issues has an impact on the university students' success during field experiences, and each topic is delivered in practical and applicable terms. Book IV, *Emerging Trends in Teacher Preparation: The Future of Field Experiences*, addresses areas of special interest affecting field experiences: (a) the promotion of reflective practices throughout all field experiences in teacher preparation programs; (b) the multicultural classroom environments education students will have to face; (c) the effective utilization of technology in field experience programs; (d) the awareness of legal ramifications of policies, or the lack of them, in field experience programs; (e) the development of leadership potential in preservice teachers; (f) the support for the first year on the job; and (g) the special opportunities for student teaching field experiences abroad. A new look at the psychology of supervision is also presented, along with a view of how the past can help us shape the future in field experiences. At the end of each book, there is a chapter titled "Bits and Pieces" that presents other issues that are critical to the overall success of field experience programs. Key points mentioned in each book are synthesized and analyzed. The information is presented in a somewhat encapsulated view, along with additional points that may need mentioning.

The composite focus of all four books in the series is to provide the information and operational examples to assist others in offering strong, challenging, and viable field experience programs throughout the country. The reader will find that each topic addressed in all the books will place an emphasis on the practical application of the ideas and information presented. The series of books will provide readers not only with "food for thought" but also "food for action."

Acknowledgments

A massive project like this is possible only because of many wonderful people contributing their expertise, time, and energy into making it happen. From all over the country friends and colleagues worked diligently to contribute a special piece to one of the books. My sincere appreciation to my authors who patiently worked with me to complete this series.

Thanks also go to my office staff, Tina Holmes and Diane Ross, and to my university supervisors, Drs. Donna Garvey, Tammie Brown, Betsy Ward, and Ed Lundin, who kept the office running smoothly while I labored over "the books," as they came to be known in the office. Our office teamwork and philosophy of operation paid off during this project. Thanks go to my graduate assistants, Leslie Peebles and Amy Palughi, whose hard work during the initial stages of this project launched us with a good beginning. Most especially thanks go to Mrs. Lauree Mills Mooney, whose organizational and computer skills made it possible for the project to be pulled together in a timely manner. Mrs. Mooney's resourcefulness in overcoming obstacles and dedication toward completing the project were invaluable. In the final stages of proofing and indexing all the books, I want to thank Ms. Holly Henderson for her timely and critical assistance.

Thanks to special friends who encouraged me throughout the project: Dr. Margaret Smith, Dr. Kenneth Burrett, Dr. Chuck Jaquith, and Dr. Sandra Gupton.

The timely production and final completion of all four books could not have occurred without the kind and caring encouragement and guidance of the Corwin Press staff. My sincere thanks go to Alice Foster, Marlene Head, Wendy Appleby, Susan McElroy, and Lin Schonberger for their understanding and patience throughout this project.

A special thanks to my husband, Sam Slick, for his constant encouragement and support. Also, special thanks to my children, Andrew and Samantha, who patiently tiptoed around the house so Mom could think and compose in order to finish "the books"!

About the Contributors

Genevieve Brown, currently a professor and chair of Educational Leadership and Counseling at Sam Houston State University, formerly served as coordinator of secondary education and supervisor of student teachers at SHSU. Previously, she was a middle and high school teacher and served in various administrative roles in public schools, including 10 years as assistant superintendent for curriculum and instruction. A frequent presenter at state and national conferences and author of several articles on teacher effectiveness, curriculum and instruction, and leadership, she was recently named the Outstanding Instructional Leader in Texas and Outstanding Woman Educator in the state.

Kenneth Burrett is a professor in the school of education at Duquesne University and an associate in the center for character education, civic responsibility, and teaching. He also serves as a charter faculty member for Duquesne University's Interdisciplinary Doctoral Program for Education Leaders. A former elementary and secondary teacher and high school department chair, he has served as director of student teaching and associate dean at Duquesne. He received his bachelor of arts and master of science degrees from Canisius College and his Ed.D. from the State University of New York at Buffalo. He is active in Phi Delta Kappa, the Pennsylvania Association of Colleges and Teacher Educators (PAC-TE), and the Association for Teacher Educators (ATE). He was named Teacher Educator of the Year in 1989 by the Pennsylvania Unit of ATE. He serves on the board of Conservation Consultants, a nonprofit environmental organization; is past president of Western Pennsylvania Council for the Social Sciences; and serves on the board of PAC-TE and various committees of ATE. He has also secured numerous grants for inservicing veteran science teachers and encouraging career change individuals to enter teaching. This past year he coauthored a book chapter and *Phi Delta Kappa Fastback*, both concerned with integrated character education. He has also delivered numerous papers in the area of leadership theory and program design.

Arthur L. Costa is Emeritus Professor of Education at California State University, Sacramento. He served as a classroom teacher, a curriculum consultant, an assistant superintendent for instruction, and the director of educational programs for the National Aeronautics and Space Administration. He has conducted workshops thoughout the United States, Canada, Mexico and Central America, the Middle East, Australia, New Zealand, Africa, Europe, Asia, and the South Pacific. Author of numerous articles, he edited the book *Developing Minds: A Resource Book for Teaching Thinking*; authored *The Enabling Behaviors, Teaching for Intelligent Behaviors*, and *The School as a Home for the Mind*; and coauthored *Cognitive Coaching, A Foundation for Renaissance Schools*, and *The Role of Assessment in the Learning Organization: Shifting the Paradigm*. Active in many professional organizations, he served as president of both the California Affiliate as well as the National Association for Supervision and Curriculum Development.

H. Jerome Freiberg is a professor of education in the College of Education at the University of Houston and is senior research associate at Temple University for the National Center on Education in the Inner Cities. He has devoted most of the past 20 years to improving the quality of life for children, teachers, and administrators in the inner cities. He has published nearly 100 scholarly works, including articles in national and international journals, chapters, and books. He is editor of the *Journal of Classroom Interaction*, an international journal with subscribers in more than 50 nations. Two of his recent books are *Universal Teaching Strategies* (with Amy Driscoll) and *Touch the Future* (with Robert Houston, Rene Clift, and Alan Warner). His most recent publication, coauthored with Carl Rogers, is a new edition of *Freedom to Learn*. He is in *Who's Who in American Education* and was the recipient of the 1988-89 University of Houston Teaching Excellence Award and the College of Education Award for Teaching Excellence. He developed the first Teachers' Academy and Institute in Preston County, West Virginia; founded the Providence Free School for Teachers; and directed the Teacher Corps in Houston, Texas. His efforts in schools emphasize creating person-centered learning environments, including ways school and classroom management can work for the benefit of students and teachers. He was the director at Houston for the National Center on Education in the Inner Cities and the Institute for Research on Urban Schooling, chair of the College of Education faculty, and associate chair for the Department of Curriculum and Instruction. He also was a volunteer teacher at a maximum security prison.

Sandra Lee Gupton is an assistant professor with the Department of Educational Leadership in the College of Education and Psychology at the University of Southern Mississippi, where she has been for the past 3 years. Before coming to the university, she worked for over 20 years in public schools in Georgia and North Carolina as teacher, principal, assistant superintendent, and superintendent of schools. Since coming to USM, where she teaches courses in educational leadership, personnel administration, and curriculum development, she has published several book and journal articles related to her research interests in organizational leadership and the issues concerning underrepresentation of women in school administration.

Scott Hopkins is a professor and chair of the Department of Curriculum and Instruction, University of South Alabama. He has 10 years' experience as a public school teacher in elementary and middle schools, and 19 years' experience as a teacher educator in three states. His areas of expertise include working with school-based teacher educators, supervision, interrelated field experiences, and teacher education program development through sequential field experiences.

Beverly J. Irby received her Ed.D. in curriculum and instruction from the University of Mississippi. Over the past 18 years she has been an elementary and middle school teacher, school psychologist, educational diagnostician, special education director, elementary school principal, director of field experiences, assistant superintendent, and interim superintendent of schools. She is a researcher of women's leadership issues as well as of science and gifted education. She is a member of the International Who's Who of Women and has received the Texas Council of Women School Executives' Outstanding Educator Award. She is the co-editor of a book on women in leadership and coauthor of two books on teen pregnancy and parenting.

Rafael Lara-Alecio is assistant professor and director of the Bilingual and English as a Second Language Programs in the College of Education, Texas A&M University at College Station, Texas. He is a native of Guatemala and a graduate of the Universidad de San Carlos and the Universidad del Valle located in Guatemala. At the Universidad de San Carlos he held several positions over a 10-year period: director of the Pedagogy Center, College of Humanities and Education; director of National Education Programs throughout Guatemala (certification and endorsement); director of field experiences; and president of Universidad de San Carlos—East Campus. In public schools he taught elementary and secondary levels and was a teacher and teacher-trainer in rural Mayan schools. He is currently a principal investigator of several training and model/demonstration grants and also researches, publishes, and presents nationally on the topics of bilingual, ESL, and multicultural issues.

James M. Mahan developed, for Indiana University, five cultural immersion projects. For 22 years, he prepared teacher certification candidates for the cultures, economic and social conditions, and education opportunities within Mexican border, American Indian reservation, overseas nation, urban, and rural communities. He then placed them in schools, social service agencies, and community homes in this group of diverse cultural settings and journeyed each semester to placement sites to evaluate their 18-week student teaching and community work performance.

Julie Fisher Mead received her doctorate in educational administration from the University of Wisconsin-Madison. She has experience as a public school teacher and administrator. While a teacher, she worked with many university students involved in field experiences. She currently lives in the San Francisco Bay Area, where she works as an educational consultant. Her special interests include special education administration and school law.

Emilio Rendon is a doctoral student in the Department of Curriculum and Instruction, College of Education, Texas A&M University. His areas of specialization include bilingual and multicultural education. He has been a classroom teacher in middle and high school, a mentor teacher, and a supervisor for student teachers. He received his B.A. from Southwest Texas State University and his M.A. in Multidisciplinary Studies at Incarnate Word College, San Antonio, Texas. He has received honors in multicultural education, including effective teaching of the Holocaust.

Joan P. Sebastian is an assistant professor of special education at the University of Utah. She has major responsibility for the coordination of the distance teacher education program for the department. Much of her experience in teacher education has been specifically in the development of a rural field-based program. Her research interests include evaluating the effectiveness of distance education teacher education programs, issues in the delivery of services for rural students with disabilities, and the evaluation of school reform proposals on rural schools.

Gloria Appelt Slick, a native of Houston, Texas, completed her doctoral work at the University of Houston in 1979. Her professional career in public school education has included classroom teaching, supervision, the principalship, and assistant superintendency for curriculum. In her current position as a faculty member of the Department of Curriculum and Instruction and as Director of Educational Field Experiences at The University of Southern Mississippi in Hattiesburg, Mississippi, her past public school experiences have provided her with significant insight into the circumstances and needs of public schools for well-trained beginning teachers. During her tenure as Director of Field Experiences, Dr. Slick has produced, in conjunction with Mississippi Educational Television, the first interactive distance learning program to deal with the subject of field experiences, titled "From Student to Teacher." These four programs were aired nationally in March 1993 and received the Mississippi Public Education Forum Award for Excellence that same year. Dr. Slick is currently president of the National Field Directors' Forum, affiliated with the Association of Teacher Educators. She also serves on the editorial board of *The Teacher Educator*. Her current research interests center on teacher preparation programs and, in particular, the interface of field experiences with those programs. Technological integration into the field experience programs and field experiences abroad are also high on her list of research and programmatic implementation.

Laura L. Stachowski has served for 13 years as the coordinator of the Overseas Student Teaching Project at Indiana University. Her responsibilities have included extensive supervision of student teachers in Indiana, Great Britain, and Ireland. Having recently completed her dissertation (*Realities Constructed by International Student Teachers*) and doctorate at Indiana University, she has been named to succeed Professor Emeritus James Mahan as director of Cultural Immersion Student Teaching Projects.

Julie K. Underwood is associate dean in the School of Education and is a professor in the School of Law at the University of Wisconsin-Madison, where in 1994 she received the Steiger Award for Excellence in Teaching. She has served as legal counsel for Herbert J. Grover, former state superintendent for the Wisconsin Department of Public Instruction, in the litigation involving the Milwaukee Parental Choice Program. She also represents school districts in Wisconsin, particularly on special education litigation.

She has served on the board of directors for the National Organization on Legal Problems of Education and the Council of School Attorneys. Her research focus is legal theories of students' rights, finance litigation, and special education. She has written a number of articles, chapters in books, and monographs. Books she has written include *Legal Aspects of Special Education and Pupil Services* (with Julie Mead) and *Handbook for Principals: Current Issues in School Law* (with William Camp).

Introduction

GLORIA APPELT SLICK

Critical issues facing teacher education in the future, in particular field experiences, are presented in *Emerging Trends in Teacher Preparation: The Future of Field Experiences*. One very critical area that must be addressed in teacher preparation is adequate training for preservice teachers in multicultural education. Providing preservice teachers with pertinent field experiences that will prepare them to function effectively as teachers in diverse class settings is very important. This diverse classroom consists not only of children representing various cultures but also of children with special needs and capabilities. As the population of the country becomes increasingly diverse and we strive to include those children with special needs into the regular classroom, the teacher becomes more responsible for modeling and teaching children how to live and function effectively in the global community in which they live. Field experience programs must provide preservice teachers with opportunities to experience and learn about the diverse composition of the classes of children they will teach.

Teachers are becoming involved in site-based management decisions as traditional top-down decision making makes way for bottom-up leadership in the public schools. To prepare teachers for their role in participatory management at their schools, field experiences should provide opportunities for preservice teachers to engage in consensus-building, problem-solving, and decision-making activities. Preservice teachers will need to shadow administrators and lead teachers who are engaged in such activities. Classroom interaction in the university setting will need to model participatory management via instructional activities involving problem-solving, consensus-building, and decision-making skills.

Technology should be utilized to the fullest in field experiences. E-mail can serve students and their supervisors as an easily accessible network for interactive dialogue. Compressed video can provide distance learning possibilities for students in remote locations. Videotapes of students' preservice teaching abilities should be included in portfolios. Individual computers for teacher use in the classroom should be the norm. Word processing, desktop publishing, data entry, bookkeeping, scheduling, and more should be accessible to the classroom teacher with a personal computer. The world can come into the classroom with Internet and such contemporary, knowledge-based programs as *Prodigy*. The profession should embrace the technology available for instructional and organizational purposes. Then it should provide preservice teachers with experiences that allow them to acquire the skills to effectively utilize that technology. Further uses of technological advantages in field experiences are described in this book. Particular reference is made to uses during student teaching.

In our litigious society, awareness of legal responsibilities in the workplace is extremely important for the classroom teacher. Field experience programs need to provide opportunities for preservice teachers to become acutely aware of legal issues related to their future jobs as teachers. Students should be encouraged to become members of professional organizations that carry liability insurance.

Emerging Trends in Teacher Preparation: The Future of Field Experiences also presents information about international field experiences. These experiences enrich the students' lives and perspectives about the topics they teach in their classes. After student teaching in a foreign country, students are better prepared to teach in a diversified classroom.

Throughout the series, the issue of reflective practices continues to surface. In this final book, this characteristic of an effective teacher is explored in depth. The past practices of field experience programs are reviewed and used to gain insight for future practices. The first year of teaching is viewed in terms of the level of preparation the neophyte teacher feels he or she has obtained during teacher preparation, and specifically as a result of field experiences. Finally, the reader is provided a description of the new psychology of supervision, which encompasses four phases of instructional thought. A description of the supervisor's mission in relationship to the phases of instructional thought is also provided.

Within this book a vision for the future of field experiences is provided that is grounded in reflective practices. The challenge of field experience programs of the future will be to incorporate all the critical issues facing the profession into meaningful, relevant clinical experiences that allow preservice teachers to apply their knowledge and skills as practicing professionals.

Using the Past;
Guiding the Future

SCOTT HOPKINS

The Past

For preservice teachers, field experiences are the critical step in becoming professional educators. These field experiences offer opportunities for preservice teachers to meld theory into practice through application of concepts, principles, and ideals gleaned from instructional specialists in institutions of higher education. The culminating field experience, commonly called student teaching, should be the integrative capstone of a teacher preparation program.

Field experiences have undergone considerable change over the years as the knowledge base of teacher preparation has expanded. They have moved from the apprenticeship era to the normal school era, to the teacher's college era, and to the beginnings of collaborative arrangements between institutions of higher education and schools.

The original field experience in teacher preparation was the apprenticeship. Preservice teachers were indentured to a school master to learn the profession. The apprentice did not receive a liberal arts education or study subjects in depth. The approach was essentially that of practicing the craft until the apprentice was deemed a qualified teacher. Later, the normal school began to emerge, between 1829 and 1900. Their programs consisted of a 2-year course of study culminating in one field experience in a model school associated with the normal school. In this model for present-day practices, preservice teachers were placed in the normal school to observe, study, and practice the art of teaching. If students spent enough hours applying theory in the model school classroom, the foundation for effective instructional practices had been established.

In the early 1900s normal schools established laboratory schools with convenient access for preservice teachers at the university. These schools, often the school of children of university professors, were the "best" schools in the district and not representative of local schools. Additionally, there were several university students assigned to one teacher, resulting in limited teaching experiences and interaction with students.

As society began to change in the 1950s and 1960s, teacher educators recognized that the laboratory school approach to field experiences was not producing teachers equipped to teach in schools reflective of a changing society. The focus of field experiences originated with a concern that initial field experiences were occurring too late in the program. Preservice teachers were encouraged, and then required, to start the initial field experience as part of the introductory phase of professional education. This led to programs requiring field experiences earlier in the program, which improved career commitment (Applegate, 1985) and preservice teachers' ability to demonstrate methods course pedagogy (Sunal, 1980). Once preservice teachers began to participate in field experiences earlier in the program, institutions began to focus upon the total number of hours spent in field experiences. As this increase in hours revealed more success, this anticipated improvement centered on how time was spent in field experiences. Subsequent development led to a concentration on activities that offered potential for learning teacher responsibilities. This involved observing, tutoring, writing about experiences, noninstructional tasks, media use, evaluating student activities, and designing instructional materials for students. Refinement of these activities resulted in identifying specific activities as being field components in specific courses. In an attempt to integrate theory and practice, these components were often associated with particular courses. The integration of field experiences with a specific class is more common in elementary schools than secondary schools and encourages reflective thought (Hill, 1986) and increases performance in subsequent courses (Denton, 1982). The structure allowed students to gain and increase their responsibility as they progressed through the program. This demonstrated the value of field experience as a learning activity for the culminating field experience, student teaching, and gave credence to the differentiation of activities based upon the level of field experience (Moore, Tullis, & Hopkins, 1990). The greatest change in field experience was one of vision. Rather than providing the opportunity to practice, field experiences were viewed as a time for preservice teachers to question, inquire, probe, and experiment. This meant the very nature of the experience, as well as the characteristics for choosing the site and school personnel, had to be changed. Rather than select teachers who could model desirable instructional strategies according to a preconceived model acceptable to the university, teachers for field experience students had to be reflective practicitioners, capable of dialogue and communion with students and preservice teachers, capable of implementing the best of practice.

The Present

Field experiences are in transition. They are beginning to move toward a conceptual model that provides examples of best practice. Goodlad's (1990) centers of pedagogy are not realities as part of most teacher education programs but are providing direction for institutions. Unfortunately, this direction is not being formulated by philosophical concerns and beliefs about the type of field experiences that are most beneficial to preservice teachers. Instead, the impetus is being provided by directives of accreditation agencies, convenience, and tradition instead of the most effective means of linking campus and field experience programs.

Although accreditation agencies may be viewed by some as restricting or inhibiting the growth of field experiences, they offer needed structure and consistency to field experiences. Field experiences cannot be just a series of sequential activities in schools; they must be founded in a coherent structure, called the knowledge base, that provides directions to the entire professional education activities of a unit. Until prodded by the National Council for the Accreditation of Teacher Education (NCATE), teacher educators naively assumed they and others knew, understood, and appreciated the extensiveness of knowledge required to provide meaningful field experiences. In an effort to meet the requirements of NCATE, teacher educators have been required to articulate, in very specific terms, the essence of what was used to develop, evaluate, and modify field experiences for preservice teachers. This essence determines how content, students, and learning interact with pedagogical knowledge to strengthen the quality of decisions being made in the teaching/learning environment of a field experience.

The prominence of field experiences in accreditation is further exemplified by the role activities related to field experiences have in the preparation of an institutional report for NCATE. Of the 95 criteria, 18 standards, and five categories, 15 criteria (24 through 38), 3 standards (II.A through II.C), and one category (Relationship to the World of Practice) focus upon field experiences. This emphasis upon field experiences has begun to make administrators aware that the success of a unit's NCATE visit is dependent upon a quality field experience as part of an inclusive teacher education program.

The selection and involvement of school personnel in field experiences has progressed from earlier ideas that all teachers needed to do was have good discipline and they could work with preservice teachers. Research has verified the importance of classroom management skills of teachers but has also indicated that just as there are requisite skills for working with students, there are skills for working with adult preservice teachers. Although being an excellent teacher and role model is essential for those assigned to work with preservice teachers, other characteristics are also essential. These teachers must be willing to be role models to assist the preservice teachers through encouragement, guidance, observation, cooperation, and openness.

The process of evaluating preservice teachers' successes in field experiences has taken a more pragmatic approach. Initially, the approach was toward summative evaluation, with the emphasis upon the grade assigned by the university supervisor. The goal of this process was to be a sorter, with identifiable documentation that supported the sorting process through the assignment of a specific grade. This process did little to encourage the involvement of preservice teachers in evaluation. A formative approach to evaluation, with the goal of feedback to facilitate growth, encourages preservice teachers to reflect upon their experiences by examining their own successes and areas of needed growth. This change in emphasis assists the preservice teacher by focusing upon skills necessary for success at all levels of field experience. This movement away from a neotraditionalist approach to supervision, with its emphasis upon observing specific behaviors in preservice teachers during field experiences, encourages preservice teachers to assume an increased share of responsibility as they progress through field experiences. As active participants in their own evaluation, preservice teachers approach evaluation with less anxiety and should recognize it as an opportunity to improve.

The Future

Society and the schools have continued to change much faster than the ability of institutions in charge of preparing teachers. Hampered by bureaucratic rules of states and the static resistance of faculty, many teacher education programs are preparing teachers for schools of the 1980s. If the schools are to be improved, teacher educators, schools, and states must allow the development of field experiences that meet the needs of the students while providing maximum opportunities for preservice teachers to develop the skills, abilities, and attitudes necessary for success as teachers in the 21st century.

In order for field experiences to become the zenith of preservice teacher preparation, the most important characteristic is the recognition of the importance of field experience. Field experiences are when preservice teachers have the opportunity to demonstrate what teaching is all about. Any focus, except where teachers practice their craft, diminishes the function of a teacher education program. The value of field experiences must go beyond verbal assurances into a realistic commitment of time, energy, focus, and financial resources of the institution preparing teachers. The goal of faculty in teacher education should be to work with preservice teachers in schools. This means novice teacher educators could only be assigned to teach classes; once they gained advanced rank and/or tenure, they would be allowed to work in the schools representing the institution and teacher educators. This may be the reverse of practices at most institutions. However, when a university makes this type of commitment to its field experience program, other types of problems will be diminished by the institutional commitment, and the true worth of field experiences will be exemplified.

True collaboration will be the hallmark of field experiences. The category of teacher educators will be expanded to consist of university-based teacher educators and school-based teacher educators. Comprehensive, sequential, and structured field experiences will be developed and arranged by university-based and school-based teacher educators. As part of the arrangement, the qualifications of school personnel will be jointly developed. Those teacher educators working in schools know the characteristics of teachers who would be successful working with preservice teachers in field experiences, and this expertise should be utilized. This group will be a natural outgrowth of the collaborative arrangement that developes a knowledge base as well as the objectives of the field experience program. This activity will empower teachers with a sense of control over the profession while encouraging them to serve as role models for future teachers. Such opportunities will also assist preservice teachers in becoming the type of empowered teachers necessary for tomorrow's schools.

The very nature of field experiences offers the greatest hope to improve the schools. Those with most expertise regarding the teaching/learning process and how it should be implemented are university faculty who have spent their professional careers studying this process. Rather than remain at the university, teaching preservice teachers how to improve the instructional practices in the school, these experts should be provided the opportunity to work in the schools and demonstrate their craft. This demonstration of structuring teaching/learning to present the best practice will enhance the quality of the schools while also demonstrating to the public that teacher educators are practicitioners of the best teaching strategies and manifesting the importance of field experiences.

Authentic assessment will be a characteristic of field experiences in the future. Too often assessment models in teacher education are associated with activities that may not be directly related to field experience activities. Authentic assessment uses a variety of sources that provide a comprehensive picture of the preservice teacher's interactions with students, school personnel, and parents. Developmental and sequential growth will be documented as the preservice teacher completes successive field experiences. Among the contents of a portfolio are videotapes, lesson plans, evidence of successful instructional strategies, reflective journals, plans for professional growth, self-evaluations, and other assessments that provide a total picture of the preservice teacher. Assessment will be part of the overall schemata developed through the collaboration between university-based teacher educators and school-based teacher educators and will be related to the total field experience program.

Reflective teachers are essential for schools of the 21st century. Preservice teachers must have field experiences that free them from impulsive and routine activities. Field experiences must provide structure and encouragement for preservice teachers to think about a subject and give it serious and consecutive consideration so they may act in a deliberate and intentional manner. Nonreflective preservice teachers rely on routine behavior guided by impulse, tradition, and authority, which limits them to concentrating their efforts on finding the most effective and efficient means to achieve ends and solve problems that have been defined for them by others. In contrast, reflective preservice teachers consistently and carefully consider and reconsider beliefs and practices evolving from these beliefs. This does not mean that field experiences should encourage preservice teachers to live without some constraints, but rather that they not accept institutional constraints as being predetermined by authority or tradition. Field experiences for preservice teachers should allow them to act in deliberate and intentional ways, to devise new ways of teaching rather than being slaves to conventional practice, and to use field experiences as a basis for professional growth.

Field experiences are the most maligned and most valued part of teacher education. Theoreticians and practicitioners agree that quality field experiences produce quality beginning teachers. Conversely, field experiences that limit preservice teachers to constrictive roles produce beginning teachers without a vision, predestined to spend years engaging in robotic actions that provide their students with less than the best. Unfortunately, university-based teacher educators have only themselves to blame. Their reluctance to make personal and professional commitments to the demands of field experiences have resulted in shallow field experiences that are field experiences only in name. Teaching is a demanding, complex activity that requires deliberate thought based upon careful analysis of situational variables. The only places that can offer preservice teachers the opportunity to develop these analytical skills are field experience sites. Interest in improving the preservice program offers the opportunity for university-based teacher educators to make significant progress toward improving the schools of the 21st century by improving the quality of field experiences. The opportunity awaits our actions.

References

Applegate, J. H. (1985). Early field experiences: Three viewpoints. In M. Haberman & J. M. Backus (Eds.), *Advances in teacher education* (Vol. 3, pp. 75-93). Norwood, NJ: Ablex.

Denton, J. (1982). Early field experience influence on performance in subsequent coursework. *Journal of Teacher Education, 33*(2), 19-23.

Goodlad, J. S. (1990). *Teachers for our nation's schools.* San Francisco: Jossey-Bass.

Hill, S. E. (1986). Language education and field experiences. *Journal of Teacher Education, 37*(3), 56-59.

Moore, K., Tullis, R., & Hopkins, S. (1990) Field experiences: Expectations versus reality. *The Teacher Educator, 26*(1), 15-22.

Sunal, D. (1980). Effects of field experiences during elementary methods courses on preservice teacher behavior. *Journal of Research in Science Teaching, 17*(1), 17-23.

The New Psychology
of Supervision

ARTHUR L. COSTA

As American schools transform themselves to meet the needs
of education for the information age and beyond, so, too, must
there be a renaissance in supervision. This chapter contains significant new concepts and functions of supervision in the profession as a whole and in field experiences specifically.

Five fresh assumptions are illuminated and five internal human
drives that motivate human cognition and action are described.
Based upon those assumptions and drives, the new role of supervision is illuminated. (These concepts are derived from Costa &
Garmston, 1994. Permission by the publisher and coauthor to
draw on these materials is greatly appreciated.)

Five Assumptions

1. *All behavior is rational and is the result of internal maps and perceptions.* What teachers do in the classroom is determined by their perceptions of their role, their knowledge about and repertoire of instructional strategies, and their knowledge of their students and how they learn, as well as about the structure of the discipline of knowledge they are responsible for teaching. To install, alter, or refine instructional behaviors, supervisors must mediate by inviting teachers to become aware of and to evaluate their perceptions and cognitive maps of their own reality.

2. *Teaching is decision making.* We are coming to understand that the act of teaching is a highly intellectual process involving continuous decision making—before, during, and after classroom instruction. Certain invisible, cognitive skills drive teaching performance. These teacher thought processes influence their classroom behaviors, students' classroom behaviors, student achievement, and, reciprocally, the teacher's thought processes, theories, and beliefs. The overt behaviors we observe in classroom performance are the results and artifacts of invisible decisions and complex intellectual processes in the teacher's mind (Joyce & Showers, 1988).

Richard Shavelson (1976) states: "Any teaching act is the result of a decision, whether conscious or unconscious, that the teacher makes after the complex cognitive processing of available information. This reasoning leads us to the hypothesis that *the basic teaching skill is decision making.*" These thought processes are influenced by deeply buried theories of learning, beliefs about education and student conduct, and the teacher's cognitive styles. Supervisors can raise these deep-structure forms of knowing to a more conscious level so the teacher can elaborate, clarify, evaluate, and alter them.

3. *These invisible cognitive skills can be categorized in four phases.* *Preactive* thought occurs as the teacher is planning before teaching. *Interactive* thought occurs during teaching. *Reflective thought* occurs as a teacher recalls and analyzes a lesson. *Projective thought*

involves synthesizing learnings and planning next steps. (These four phases of thought will be elaborated below.)

4. To learn anything well requires the engagement and transformation of the mind. Based on this cognitive perception of teaching, we regard the mediational role of the supervisor as a process of engaging, enhancing, and transforming the intellectual functions of teaching. A supervisor can fulfill this role by eliciting how and what teachers are thinking as they plan for, execute, evaluate, and construct meaning from their instructional experiences.

If we believe that teaching is an intellectual process of decision making, and the work of teaching is the application of cognitive processes, then the supervision and evaluation of teaching should be enhancement and assessment of decision making. This view, along with the other changes in efforts to restructure schools, constitutes yet another paradigm shift in personnel policies and procedures.

5. Professional adults are capable of continual intellectual growth and learning throughout their lifetimes. Beginning teachers may not assume their first teaching assignments as autonomous professionals, and some veteran teachers may experience situations in which their resourcefulness is at a low ebb. Continual teacher growth occurs developmentally and individually over time. Continual intellectual growth is influenced and supported through mediated learning experiences from a variety of sources: from skilled staff developers, graduate course work, reading, collaboration with peers, modeling by others whom the teacher has grown to respect, by the subtle cues emanating from the school culture, and by the new teacher's critical friend and mentor, the supervisor.

Teachers have implicit theories about teaching and learning that are "robust, idiosyncratic, sensitive to their particular experiences, incomplete, familiar, and sufficiently pragmatic to have gotten them to where they are today" (Clark & Peterson, 1986). By talking aloud about these internal maps, supervisors can cause teachers to examine, refine, and develop new theories and practices. Through supervisory discussions about the reasoning behind their actions and responding to questions about their perceptions and teaching decisions, teachers often experience a sense of professional excitement and renewed joy and energy related to their work. The supervisor, therefore, will invite teachers to disclose their thinking and decisions about teaching, because it not only energizes teachers, it also causes them to refine their cognitive maps, and hence their instructional choices and behaviors. Furthermore, it creates an image, especially for beginning teachers, of their chosen profession as an intellectually challenging, growth producing, complex, and dignified profession. Teachers, in turn, will more likely create similar visions of classroom interactions with their students. Some of the cognitive processes that might become the subject of such teacher-supervisory dialogue are described below.

Four Phases of Instructional Thought

Goal-directed teaching consists of four rather distinct stages: (1) planning for action, (2) monitoring during practice, (3) reflection on practice, and (4) projecting ahead. *Planning* (the preactive phase) consists of all the intellectual functions performed before instruction. *Teaching* (the interactive phase) includes the multiple decisions made during teaching. *Analyzing and evaluating* (the reflective phase) consists of all those mental processes used to think back on, analyze, and judge instruction. Finally, *applying* (the projective phase) involves constructing meaning by abstracting from the experience, synthesizing new generalizations, and applying them to future situations. Major cognitive functions within each of these phases are described below.

The Cognitive Processes of Planning: The Preactive Phase

Planning may well include the most important decisions teachers make because it is the phase upon which all other decisions rest. Planning basically involves four components (Shavelson, 1976):

1. Anticipating, envisioning, predicting, and developing precise descriptions of students' learnings that are to result from instruction.

2. Identifying students' present capabilities or entry knowledge. This information is drawn from previous teaching/learning experience, data from school records, test scores, and clues from previous teachers, parents, and counselors (Borko, Cone, Russo, & Shavelson, 1979).

3. Envisioning precisely the characteristics of an instructional sequence or strategy that will most likely move students from their present capabilities toward immediate and long-range instructional outcomes. This sequence is derived from whatever theories, beliefs, or models of teaching logic, learning, or motivation that the teacher has adopted. The sequential structure of a lesson is deeply embedded in teachers' plans for allocating that precious and limited resource: time.

4. Anticipating a method of assessing outcomes. The outcomes of this assessment will provide a basis for evaluating and making decisions about the design of the next cycle of instruction.

The human intellect has a limited capacity for handling variables. Miller (1963) describes this as "M-space" or Memory Space. He found that humans have a capacity for handling and coordinating seven different variables, decisions, or disparate pieces of information at any one time (plus or minus two). When humans approach the outer limits of their capacity, a state of stress begins to set in, and there's a feeling of loss of control. As teachers gain experience, their intellectual energy appears to be invested in techniques and systems to simplify, reduce, and select the number of variables. Certain planning strategies help reduce this stress and should become the focus of the supervisory process.

During planning, a teacher envisions cues—definitions of acceptable forms of student performance for learning. This simplifies judgments about appropriate and inappropriate student behaviors. The teacher also selects potential solutions, back-up procedures, and alternative strategies for times when the activity needs to be redirected, changed, or terminated.

Planning causes thought experiments during which a teacher can mentally rehearse activities to help anticipate possible events and consequences. This improves the coordination and efficiency of subsequent performance, because systematic mental rehearsal prepares the mind and body for the activity and is the main mechanism for focusing attention on critical factors relevant to the task.

When a person thinks about an action, the brain sends impulses to the nerves and muscles in the corresponding locations of the mind and body associated with the action. This is called the "Carpenter Effect" (Ulich, 1967) and is the scientific basis for the practice of mental rehearsal. Through mental rehearsal, we learn to direct attention to cues that are most important for performance and at the same time close down the perceptions of distracting external stimuli. During the planning phase, therefore, it is helpful to rehearse entire lesson sequences (Jansson, 1983).

Planning also demands that the teacher exercise perceptual flexibility—viewing learning from multiple perspectives. This requires a certain degree of detachment from the instruction in order to stand off and assume alternative perspectives. Highly flexible teachers have the capacity to view their lesson in both the immediate and the long range. They are not only analytical about the details of this lesson (the micro mode), they also can see connections between this lesson and other related learnings. They know where this lesson is leading and how it is connected to broader curricular goals (the macro mode). Less flexible, episodic teachers may view today's activity as a separate and discrete episode, unrelated to other learning events.

Flexible teachers see a lesson from a variety of points of view. The teacher may view the lesson *egocentrically*—from his own point of view, including his goals, teaching strategies, and content background; *allocentrically*—from a student's point of view; *macrocentrically*—imagining how the entire interaction will appear from a mental "balcony," overlooking the interactions between teacher and students; and *retrocentrically*—envisioning the end or completed product and backing up from that vision to form strategies and steps of how to achieve the vision.

Planning a teaching strategy also requires analysis, both structural and operational. Structural analysis is the process of breaking down the learning of the content into its component parts; operational analysis involves a seriation of events into a logical order of sequence (Clark & Yinger, 1979). To handle this information overload, teachers probably synthesize much of this information into "hypotheses" or best guesses about student readiness for learning. They estimate the probability of successful student behavior as a result of instruction.

Shavelson (1976) believes that of the four phases of teachers' thought, planning is the most important because it sets the standard for the remaining three phases. Also of great value seems to be specifying clear learning objectives. The more clearly the teacher envisions and mentally rehearses the plan, the greater the chance that the lesson will achieve its purposes, the more likely the teacher will self-monitor his or her own actions and decisions during the lesson, and the more likely the teacher will critically analyze his or her own lesson during the reflective phase, thereby assuming a greater internal locus of control.

The Cognitive Processes of Teaching: The Interactive Phase

Teaching has been described as the second most stressful profession. This stems from the fact that teachers are constantly interacting with students in an environment of uncertainty (Harvey, 1966). Teachers are constantly making decisions that may be subconscious, spontaneous, planned, or a mixture of each. They are probably modifications of decisions made during the planning phase, but now they're carried out on the spur of the moment in the fast-paced interaction of the classroom. Changes may not be well defined or as thoroughly considered as those made during the calmer stage of planning. Teachers have little time to consider alternative teaching strategies and the consequences of each.

Teachers plan in multiple time dimensions: weekly, daily, long range, short range, yearly, and term. Effective teachers relate information from all those time frames as they prepare daily lessons (Yinger, 1977). Several temporal capacities interact constantly with teachers' thoughts and values and influence their moment to moment decisions. These may include *sequence*—the seriation or ordering of instructional events within a lesson; *simultaneity*—teaching toward multiple and varied outcomes, strategies, learning styles, and the like at the same time; *rhythm*—pacing the lesson, regulating the tempo and recurrence of learnings; and *synchronicity*—aligning the learning into allotted time constraints and schedules. (For an elaboration of teacher's temporal thought processes, refer to Appendix B in Costa & Garmston, 1994.)

Keeping a planned strategy in mind while teaching provides the teacher a backdrop against which to make new decisions. During the beginning of a lesson, for example, the teacher may emphasize structuring the task and motivating students to become curious, involved, and focused. Later in the sequence, the teacher may use recall types of thinking to review previously learned information and to gather data to be considered later. Further into the lesson, the teacher may invite higher-level thinking and, finally, tasks for transference and application.

Clark and Peterson (1986) describe the content of teachers' interactive thought related to (a) changing their plans, (b) the influences on those decisions, (c) the cues that teachers read in order to make decisions, and (d) the relationships between teachers' interactive decisions, teacher behaviors, and, ultimately, student outcomes. A relatively small portion of teachers' interactive thoughts deal with instructional objectives. A greater percentage of teachers' interactive thoughts deal with the content or subject matter. A still greater percentage of interactive thoughts deal with the instructional process, and the largest percentage of teachers' interactive thought concerns learning and the learner.

Novice teachers may suffer cognitive overload—too many things going on all at the same time—yet skillful teachers respond immediately, intuitively, and spontaneously. Highly conscious teachers are alert to what is going on in the classroom; less conscious teachers continue their lessons regardless of what occurs among the students. Alert teachers search for clues that students are learning: Has the student acted on the information, digested it, and made meaning out of it or used it? Are students staring vacantly, or do body language and facial cues indicate attention? The alert teacher constantly observes, questions, probes, and interprets students' behaviors to make decisions about moving ahead in the sequence or remaining at the present step longer.

Metacognition also refers to the ability to know what we know and what we don't know. It is our ability to plan a strategy for producing what information is needed, to be conscious of our own steps and strategies, and to reflect on and evaluate the productivity of our thinking. Metacognition in teachers is a critically important capacity to consciously stand outside and reflect on themselves as they manage instruction. During a lesson, teachers may conduct an inner dialogue asking themselves: Are my directions clear? Can students see the TV monitor? Am I using precise words to make sure that the students are understanding? Should I speed up? Such self-talk means the teacher is constantly monitoring his or her own and students' behavior during instruction.

The metacognitive skills necessary to successful teaching—and what the supervisor, therefore, may want to develop—include:

- keeping place in a long sequence of operations,
- knowing that a subgoal has been attained, and
- detecting errors and recovering from them by making a quick fix or retreating to the last known correct operation.

This kind of monitoring involves both looking ahead and looking back. Looking ahead includes:

- learning the structure of a sequence of operations and identifying areas where errors are likely,
- choosing a strategy that will reduce the possibility of error and will provide easy recovery, and
- identifying the kinds of feedback that will be available at various points and evaluating the usefulness of that feedback.

Looking back includes:

- detecting errors previously made,
- keeping a history of what has been done to the present and thereby what should come next, and
- assessing the reasonableness of the present and the immediate outcome of task performance.

As teachers monitor the classroom for conscious and subconscious cues, they sometimes build up so much information that they disrupt conscious information processing. Flexible teachers restrain their impulsivity by avoiding strong emotional reactions to classroom events. This is an efficient strategy to reserve the limited capacity for conscious processing of immediate classroom decisions.

Flexible teachers have a vast repertoire of instructional strategies and techniques and call forth alternative strategies as needed. In many classes there is a heterogeneous array of languages, cultures, and learning styles. Each must be dealt with by employing different strategies, vocabulary, examples, and techniques. Efficacious and flexible teachers continually add to and draw upon their vast repertoire for strategies that may prove effective.

Routines are helpful in dealing with the information-processing demands of the classroom. Routines reduce the need to attend to the abundance of simultaneous cues from the environment. Efficacious teachers develop a repertoire of routine systems for dealing with many classroom management functions (taking roll, distributing papers and books). They also have systematic lesson designs (e.g., spelling and math drills) and teaching strategies (e.g., questioning sequences, structuring).

The Cognitive Processes of Analyzing and Evaluating: The Reflective Phase

After teaching the lesson, the teacher now has two sources of information: the lesson that was envisioned during planning and the actual lesson as performed. Analyzing involves collecting and using understandings derived from the comparison between actual and intended outcomes. If there is a great similarity between the two, there is a match, but if a discrepancy exists between the lesson that was planned and the lesson that was taught, teachers then generate reasons to explain the discrepancies. Causal relationships between instructional situations and behavioral outcomes are generated and explored.

Teachers can either assume responsibility for their own actions or they can place the blame on external forces. Teachers with an *external locus of control* tend to misplace responsibility on situations or persons beyond their control. Efficacious teachers have an *internal locus of control*. They assume responsibility for their own successes or failures.

Even with this analysis, the cycle of instructional decision making is not yet complete. The learnings must be constructed, synthesized, and applied or transferred to other learning contexts, content areas, and life situations.

The Cognitive Processes of Applying:
The Projective Phase

In this phase, the teacher constructs new knowledge and applies that knowledge to future instructional situations or content. Experience can bring change, but experience alone is not enough. Meaning is constructed when experience is compared, differentiated, categorized, and labeled.

Skillful teachers consciously reflect upon, conceptualize, and apply understandings from one classroom experience to the next. As a result of this analysis and reflection, they synthesize new knowledge about teaching and learning. As experiences with teaching and learning accumulate, concepts are derived and constructed. As a result, teachers become more routinized, particularized, and refined. They are capable of predicting consequences of their decisions and are therefore more experimental and risk-taking. They expand their repertoire of techniques and strategies to be used in different situations with varying content and unique groups of students. Without this conceptual system, the teacher's perception of the classroom remains chaotic.

Teaching is cognitively complex. Some of the cognitive or intellectual processes involved in the four components of the instructional act have been examined. Even the myriad decisions reported here are driven by even more deeply embedded conscious or subconscious beliefs, styles, metaphors, perceptions, and habits. If teachers do not possess these mental capacities, no amount of experience alone will create it. It is through supervisory mediation that these capacities will be developed (Feuerstein & Feuerstein, 1991). As supervisors, therefore, we are interested in eliciting, enhancing, and refining the teacher's inner thought processes.

The Supervisor's Mission

Five internal psychological states of mind drive human growth toward performance of these complex cognitive abilities. These five passions or energy sources motivate human thought and action. For an individual, they represent the continuing tensions and resources for acting congruently. For an organization, they form an invisible energy field, in which all parties are affected as surely as a strong magnetic field affects a compass. Taken together, they are a force propelling humans toward increasingly authentic behavior. They are the tools of disciplined choice making. They are the primary vehicles in the lifelong journey toward personal integration.

Enhancing these five states, therefore, may be the new long-range mission of supervision. Because they are natural human drives, effective supervisors will draw upon them as resources or catalysts for their own and teachers' continued intellectual growth. The five states of mind may serve the supervisor as diagnostic tools—constructs through which we can assess the cognitive development of other individuals and groups and plan interventions. But assisting others toward refinement and expression starts first with the self, the supervisor's own states of mind. From there, it emanates to others, to the system in which the supervisor is a part, and ultimately to students.

Efficacy

Efficacious teachers have an internal locus of control. They persevere. They produce knowledge. They engage in cause-effect thinking. They pose questions and search for problems to solve. They are optimistic and resourceful. They are self-actualizing and self-modifying. They are able to operationalize concepts and translate them into deliberate actions. They establish feedback spirals and continue to learn how to learn.

Flexibility

Flexible teachers are empathic. They can see through the diverse perspectives of others. They are comfortable with ambiguity and can change their minds with the addition of new information. They use lateral thinking, are innovative and creative. They envision a range of alternative consequences. They have the capacity to change their minds as they receive additional data. They engage in multiple and simultaneous outcomes and activities and they can practice style flexibility, knowing when it is appropriate to be broad and global in their thinking and when a situation calls for precision.

Craftsmanship

Craftsmanlike teachers seek perfection and take pride in their artistry. They seek refinement and specificity in communications. They generate and hold clear visions and goals and work to align their behaviors with their goals and values. They strive for exactness of critical thought processes. They use precise language for describing their work. They manage their time effectively. They make thorough and rational decisions about instructional actions to be taken in their own classrooms. They test, revise, and constantly hone instructional strategies to reach learning goals.

Consciousness

Conscious teachers metacogitate. They monitor their own and others' values, thoughts, behaviors, and progress toward goals.

They have well-defined value systems that they can articulate. They generate, hold, and apply internal criteria for the decisions they make. They practice mental rehearsal and the editing of mental pictures in the continual process of seeking improved strategies.

Interdependence

Interdependent teachers have a sense of community. They are altruistic. They seek collegiality and give themselves to achieving group goals and needs. They value consensus and are able to hold their own thoughts and actions in abeyance in order to lend their energies to the achievement of group goals. They draw on the resources of others. They seek engagement in and reciprocity with others volunteering their services and resources to enhance the common good. They trust their abilities to manage group differences in productive ways.

The new and expanded goal of supervision in the restructuring school is to create communities of continual learners who become increasingly more efficacious, flexible, craftsmanlike, conscious, and interdependent. Renaissance supervisors will become increasingly skillful in (1) mediating all members of the school community's continued growth toward these desired states and (2) assessing the degree to which supervisors themselves and others with whom they work develop the capacity to self-analyze, self-evaluate, and self-prescribe growth toward these ends. The emerging vision of supervision, therefore, is to modify teachers' capacities to modify themselves. In that process, supervisors, too, will continue to become more efficacious, flexible, craftsmanlike, conscious, and interdependent. (For an elaboration of this form of assessment, see Costa, Garmston, & Lambert, 1988.)

References

Borko, H., Cone, R., Russo, D., & Shavelson, R. (1979). Teachers' decision making. In D. Peterson & H. Walberg (Eds.), *Research on teaching*. Berkeley, CA: McCutchan.

Clark, C., & Peterson, P. (1986). Teachers' thought processes. In M. C. Wittrock (Ed.), *Handbook of research on teaching* (3rd ed., pp. 255-296). New York: Macmillan.

Clark, C., & Yinger, R. (1979). Teachers' thinking. In D. Peterson & H. Walberg (Eds.), *Research on teaching*. Berkeley, CA: McCutchan.

Costa, A., & Garmston, R. (1994). *Cognitive coaching: A foundation for the renaissance school*. Norwood, MA: Christopher Gordon.

Costa, A., Garmston, R., & Lambert, L. (1988). Evaluation of teaching: The cognitive development view. In S. Stanley & W. J. Popham (Eds.), *Teacher evaluation: Six prescriptions for success*. Alexandria, VA: The Association for Supervision and Curriculum Development.

Feuerstein, R., & Feuerstein, S. (1991). Mediated learning experience: A theoretical review. In R. Feuerstein, P. Kelin, & A. Tannenbaum (Eds.), *Mediated learning experience (MLE) theoretical, psychosocial and learning implications*. London: Freund.

Harvey, O. J. (1966). System structure, flexibility, and creativity. In *Experience, structure, and adaptability* (pp. 39-65). New York: Springer.

Jansson, L. (1983). Mental training: Thinking rehearsal and its use. In W. Maxwell (Ed.), *Thinking: The expanding frontier*. Philadelphia: The Franklin Institute.

Joyce, B., & Showers, B. (1988). *Student achievement through staff development*. New York: Longman.

Miller, G. A. (1963, March). The magical number seven, plus or minus two: Some limits on our capacity for processing information. *Psychological Review, 2*, 81-97.

Shavelson, R. (1976). Teachers' decision making. In N. L. Gage (Ed.), *The psychology of teaching methods: 1976 yearbook of the national society for the study of education: Part I*. Chicago: University of Chicago Press.

Ulich, E. (1967). Some experiments of the function of mental training in the acquisition of motor skills. *Ergonomics, 10*, 411-419.

Yinger, R. J. (1977). *A study of teacher planning: Description and theory development using ethnographic and information processing methods*. Unpublished doctoral dissertation, Michigan State University.

❖ 3 ❖

Promoting Reflective Practices

H. JEROME FREIBERG

Knowledge is power, but knowledge about oneself is the greatest power. The power of learning and discovering about yourself as a professional is at the heart of the teaching profession, but this exploration has in the past been the jurisdiction of others. From student teaching through retirement, most teachers must rely on cooperating teachers, university supervisors, principals and district supervisors to answer the question: How am I doing? Being able to assess your own teaching will add significantly to your pedagogical knowledge. Self-assessment allows for change to occur from within. Judging the potential effects of your instruction will also expand and potentially accelerate your teaching repertoire (Freiberg & Driscoll, in press). Reflection may be defined as a quest for meaning, a metacognitive search to give context to disparate bits of information. Bailey (1981) defines teacher self-assessment as "the process of self-examination in which the teacher uses a series of sequential feedback strategies for the purpose of instructional self-improvement" (p. 9).

Barriers to Self-Assessment

Time becomes both an enhancer and a barrier to this search for meaning. Being in the midst of an event like teaching does not permit the time to reflect. Looking back later, however, when time is available, results in a loss of sharpness of the event itself. In addition to time, accurate readings of your teaching during instruction represents another barrier to meaningful self-assessment (Hook & Rosenshine, 1979). The usual classroom has nearly 1,000 interactions per hour, and sifting through fast-paced dialogues, discussions, directions, grouping, and questions challenges the most astute educator to be reflective during a typical lesson. Some reflection occurs during instruction, resulting in "in-flight corrections." These changes in teaching transpire almost instantaneously, based on a repertoire of prior experiences in similar situations (Freiberg & Driscoll, 1992). Beginning teachers have greater difficulty in this area due to a more limited repertoire of teaching experiences and options. Several studies (Anderson & Freiberg, in press; Freiberg & Waxman, 1988; Freiberg, Waxman, & Houston, 1987; Harris, 1988; Stallings, Martin, & Bossung, in press) indicate that examining and reflecting upon your teaching during field experiences can enhance the repertoire of pedagogical knowledge. The problem becomes, how do we capture the event of teaching at a later time, without losing the essence of the event?

Sources of Data

Data about yourself, according to Kremer-Hayon (1993) in her book, *Teacher Self-Evaluation: Teachers in Their Own Mirrors*, can be acquired through journals, logs, diaries, portfolios, and audio- and videotaped lessons. Accurate information about what you are doing in the classroom is needed to determine strengths and weaknesses and formulate plans for instituting change.

Although student teaching is designed to be a key clinical stage in one's professional development, the experience is often cited by beginning teachers as being negative rather than positive (Guyton & McIntyre, 1990). There are several reasons for this dissatisfaction, ranging from placement problems and lack of support to the constant reliance on others for feedback. Depending solely on outside sources for feedback about your teaching has the potential of diminishing professional efficacy and may minimize a desire for self-reflection in the future.

Observations by a cooperating teacher and university supervisor are the most common sources of data during the student teaching experience. Feedback from these sources, usually derived from observation checklists, is limited in its scope. The ephemeral frequency of observations and feedback sessions may result in few real changes in teaching practice. Other sources of data have proven to be an important basis for pedagogical development (Freiberg, Waxman, & Houston, 1987). This process of seeking instruments to capture the teaching event begins with an examination of sources of data about teaching.

Sources of data about teaching may be drawn from your daily instructional actions in terms of both what you are doing and what the students are feeling and learning. The following data sources reflect these two milieu of data opportunities:

Data Sources

Teacher	Students
Observations from other student teachers	Student written feedback on teaching practices
Observations from a supervisor or principal	Student grades during a marking period
University or cooperating teacher feedback based on videotaped lessons	Student feedback that is based on verbal or nonverbal feedback during the lesson
Self-assessment using videotape	Student achievement on teacher-made tests
Self-assessment using audiotape	Student survey feedback on learning environments

Each source can produce valuable insights; however, elements are rarely combined from both sides of the list. Self-assessment, written student feedback, and systematic classroom observations have shown to be important sources of information about your teaching. There are numerous systematic observation systems (Evertson & Burry, 1989; Flanders, 1970; Good & Brophy, 1994; Stallings & Freiberg, 1991) that may be used by cooperating teachers or university supervisors to provide you feedback on your teaching. This chapter presents two measures that can be used to capture the teaching event during real time, but may be visited at a future date when opportunities for reflection are feasible. The first self-assessment measure gathers data from audiotaping a lesson and analyzing it, based on the Low Inference Self-Assessment Measure (LISAM) (Freiberg, 1987). A second measure is derived from written student feedback during the same lesson (Freiberg & Driscoll, 1992).

LISAM[1]

The LISAM, or Low Inference Self-Assessment Measure (Freiberg, 1987), is designed to provide data on six areas of teacher-student interactions in the classroom. Some of the categories are derived from the research of Ned Flanders (1970). The LISAM uses audiotaping rather than videotaping technologies to capture verbal interactions. The "Low Inference" part of the title is derived from the phenomenon that two people listening to the same classroom recording would reach agreement on what was occurring at least 80% of the time. The LISAM (see Figure 3.1) meets many of the conditions established by Bailey (1981) for self-assessment measures. Measured against his rating scale, it has ease of operations, minimal intrusions, accessibility, portability, minimal costs, ease of use, and a permanent record, and takes less than 5 minutes to set up. You would simply tape-record your classroom for 20 to 45 minutes and listen for specific areas on the LISAM form (questioning, teacher/student talk, opening and closing of the lesson, wait-time, praise statements, and use of student ideas). The LISAM may be used in the actual classroom or in a simulated setting when you are teaching your peers. The LISAM is focused in its data collection and should be combined with other data sources, including student feedback, classroom observations, and case studies, to broaden the scope of feedback about your teaching.

Student Teacher Perceptions of the LISAM

In a study of 10 secondary student teachers who used the LISAM (Anderson & Freiberg, in press), all the students indicated the self-assessment measure was worthwhile and beneficial to their teaching.

A social studies student teacher commented:

> I think the time I invested in the LISAM is going to pay for itself in the long run. I think it's priceless, really. I mean, every student teacher should have the opportunity to look at themselves through the LISAM. Some of them I've talked to have only been observed by their college supervisor one or two times. I don't see how you could get better without the type of in-depth feedback you get from the LISAM analysis. I don't think you could get it anywhere else.

Other student teachers' subjective reactions to their use of the LISAM were also generally quite positive. The following comments were representative of the group:

> It was helpful to me to see my numbers down in black and white.

> Where you gain insights is when you do the analysis yourself. It's hard to argue with your own data.

> I never realized how many yes-no questions I did ask. It was actually going through it and putting down all those marks that made me realize what I was doing.

> Before I analyzed my tape it always seemed to me that the kids were doing most of the talking. (Note: This student

teacher talked 79.6% of the time in the lesson recorded on the first audiotape.)

I really thought I was being more divergent in my questioning, and then I listened to my tape. It's like hard facts evidence that's right there in front of you. It really opened my eyes.

I had no idea I was rushing so much until I listed to my first tape. When I timed myself it became obvious that I wasn't giving them enough time to answer.

I heard myself interrupt a thought process that was happening. A child was thinking through a problem and I took the ball away from him. I thought, "My God, how can I be doing this?" (p. 9)

The six areas of analysis on the LISAM are presented in Figure 3.1. Each of the six areas is discussed, and procedures for their use are provided.

Questioning

Questioning is the second-most used instructional strategy after lecture. Although most teachers feel they are asking thought-provoking, higher-order questions, in reality few actually ask questions that require more than factual recall. In a study of more than 1,000 questions asked by seven teachers in British elementary classrooms, E. C. Wragg (1993) reports 57% of the questions were managerial (noninstructional) in nature, 35% were lower-order recall questions, and 8% were higher-order. This pattern is very consistent with other studies that show low usage of higher-level questions (Kerry, 1987). The research is somewhat mixed when looking at using higher-level questions. A steady diet of higher-level questions may not be any better than exclusive use of lower-level questions. Questions should fit within a natural sequence in the lesson. Perhaps the best guide is to provide a balance (50/50 or 60/40) between higher- and lower-level questions. Given the

1. *Questioning Skills*   TOTAL = _____ = _____ %
   Yes-No: (Recall/Informational) TOTAL = _____ = _____ %
   Short Answer: TOTAL = _____ = _____ %
   Comparison: (Reflective/Thought   TOTAL = _____ = _____ %
                    Provoking)
   Opinions: TOTAL = _____ = _____ %

2. *Teacher Talk/Student Talk*
   Teacher: Student: Other
   Total (T) = ____ %   Total (S) = ____ %   (e.g., independent
   Teacher = ____   Student = ____   activities with no
                                                   interaction):
                                                   Total = ____ %
                                                   ____

3. *Identification of Motivating Set and Closure*
   Describe each from the tape:
       Set-Induction (Focus):
       Closure (Ending):

4. *Wait Time*
   Time between teacher question and next teacher statement:
                        Average Time = _____ Seconds
   Place a (*) next to all higher level questions (comparison and
   opinion).

5. *Identify Number of Positive Statements Made by Teacher*
   Praise or encouragement

   Class ____ Individual ____ Uses student name ____ Total = ____

   Identify the praise or encouragement statements directed both
   toward the entire class and individuals. Also tally the number of
   times students' names are used with praise statements.

6. *Identify the Number of Times Teacher Uses Student Ideas*
   Including referring by name to other student's ideas:
                                       Total = _____

Figure 3.1. Audiotape Analysis Coding Instrument
SOURCE: Adopted from Freiberg (1987). Reprinted by permission.

low levels of high-order questions, extra effort and attention will
be required to achieve the goal of balanced questioning. Writing
higher-level questions down during the lesson planning cycle is
perhaps the most effective way of achieving this goal (see Freiberg
& Driscoll, 1992).

Procedures

Listen to your tape and code your questions into one of two categories or four possible questions. The first category is composed of Factual/Recall/Informational, *Yes/No* (Is Washington, D. C., the capital of the United States?) or *Short Answer* questions (Describe how the capital city received its name.). The second category is composed of Reflective/Thought Provoking *Comparison* (How were the inaugural speeches of George Washington and John F. Kennedy similar or different?) and *Opinion* (Who was the best president of the United States?) higher-order questions. Tally the frequencies for each question, create a total for the individual question, and give a total for all questions. Calculate percentages for each question by dividing the total number for all questions into the total for each question (e.g., 13 yes/no ÷ 40 total questions = 32.5% yes/no questions).

Teacher and Student Talk

A high school Spanish teacher once told me, after analyzing her audiotape, that she was surprised her students could speak any Spanish because she talked 97% of the time. Although this figure was high, historically teachers talking in classrooms at the secondary level range between 70% and 73% in social studies classrooms, and 80% and 85% in mathematics classrooms (Brophy & Good, 1986). Although there are no clear research frameworks for the ideal percentages of teacher/student talk, instructional strategies that are less teacher-centered will produce more interaction and higher levels of student talk. Cooperative groups, discussion, roleplay, simulations, and inquiry lessons will achieve a balance between active and passive learning environments (Rogers & Freiberg, 1994).

Procedures

Listen to your tape and, using a watch with a second hand, every fifth second indicate if the ____ teacher, ____ or students are talking. On the LISAM chart if neither the teacher or students are talking, code the _____ other category. If students are talking to one another, then the student category would be coded. If students are working silently on independent seatwork, the other category would be coded. Continue this time-sampling process until the entire tape is coded. Calculate the number and percentage, using the same procedures as in the questioning section. In a 45-minute lesson, for example, you should have coded 540 frequencies of teacher, student, or other actions (45 min. × 60 sec. ÷ 5 seconds = 540 frequencies).

Identification of Motivating Set and Closure

Beginnings and endings allow for students and teachers to focus on what is to be learned and summarize what has been learned. Describe how you provided students with a focus at the beginning of the lesson. A motivating set is one in which the students are drawn into the lesson during the first few minutes. "Turn to page 36 in your book on ancient Egypt" is in stark contrast with, "I have written an ancient language on the board (Egyptian hieroglyphics); by the end of the day you will be able to translate its meaning." The first teacher statement received student compliance. The second statement received an immediate and positive reaction from the students. A study by Schuck (1985) found that biology teachers who used set inductions in their lessons had students who achieved more and retained their biology content longer than teachers who used only questioning strategies.

The use of closure allows for a lesson to be summarized and provides for linkages between elements of the lesson. It is helpful to have the students summarize the lesson. Closure will need to be part of instructional planning. Without some planning, too often the bell becomes closure for the lesson.

Procedures

Write a one-sentence description of your motivating set and your closure for the lesson.

Wait Time

Pausing to allow students time to think seems a reasonable instructional procedure. Previous research (Rowe, 1969, 1974) indicates that many teachers allow students less than 1 second to think about the question before moving to another student or rephrasing the question. Waiting 3-5 seconds for students to respond has been suggested by Rowe. But Carlsen (1991) indicates that pausing should be relevant to the context of the questions and should not be rigidly applied to all questioning situations. Perhaps the most important wait time occurs during higher-level questioning. Waiting 3-5 seconds during a fast-paced questioning exchange is less important than waiting 3-5 seconds for students to reflect on high-order questions.

There are several different types of wait time. *Wait time I* refers to the pause between a teacher question and a student response. *Wait time II* refers to the time after a student answers a question. Too often the teacher responds immediately with a comment, acknowledgment, or redirection. Waiting after a student responds encourages further interaction.

Procedures

For the LISAM, you will need to measure the time between teacher question and the next teacher statement. Place a "*" next to the higher-level questions. Use the second hand of a watch to determine the pauses between a teacher question to a student and the next teacher statement. You may have a few long pauses if the student's answer is long. The key, however, is determining how long you are pausing to allow students time to think and answer.

Identify the Number of
Positive Statements Made by the Teacher

The area of verbal praise and feedback has been one of extensive discussion. Research by Cameron and Pierce (1994) supports the importance of teacher verbal praise and positive feedback as a leading factor in improving student motivation. There is a tendency to use brief statements of praise (e.g., okay, good, yes) rather than extended and specific praise statements. These brief acknowledgments are used without variety. Praise is both a motivator and a signal to other students about the correctness of a response. Figure 3.2, titled 70 Ways to Vary Your Praise (Freiberg, 1991), is provided as an example of how variability of praise can be extended into three dimensions. The first dimension is simple acknowledgment, with words ranging from "great" to "remarkable." The second dimension is acknowledgment of specific efforts, such as "Sarah, I see you have tried very hard to complete this English assignment." The teacher is recognizing effort, although the assignment may have errors that need to be corrected. In the third area, or extended praise, the teacher statement specifies what has been accomplished. "Sarah, great job of completing your Civil War assignment. Your writing is very clear and the historical information is accurate and supports the perspective you take in the paper." You may find need of these examples as you examine your own praise and acknowledgments of your students.

Procedures

Identify and code the number of praise statements that are directed to the class, and individuals, and those which use the students' names. The more specific the statement (completion of work) and the focus (using student's name), the greater the potential for influencing student motivation.

Identify the Number of Times the Teacher Uses Student Ideas

Use of student ideas was recognized as an important motivational factor by Flanders (1970) in his research on classroom interaction. A teacher who uses student ideas is presented in the following sequence:

Science Classroom 9th grade
Teacher: Who can explain the reasons for needing a Periodic Table? Jose?

Always use the student's name in providing praise. You may *acknowledge effort, praise a positive result,* or give a *brief acknowledgment.* The following are examples of each area.

Brief Acknowledgments

OK	Sensational	Correct	Outstanding
Fine	Superb	Accurate	Standout
Great	Astonishing	Perfect	Important
Super	Incredible	True	Noteworthy
Yes	Marvelous	Precisely	Remarkable
I see	Beautiful	Truly	Notable
Nice	Grand	Agreed	Key point
Much better	Magnificent	Positively	Keep it up
Exactly	Very nice	Noted	Keep up the great work
Excellent	Dazzling	Splendid	Keep up the good work
Tremendous	Brilliant	Better	You're on target
Surely	Good	Much improved	Very nice
Right	Very Good	Superior	Congratulations

Acknowledge Specific Effort
- Bill, I like the way you are using your time to study.
- Jose, you have really focused on the lesson.
- Sarah, I see you have tried very hard to complete this English assignment.
- Don, the extra time you are spending on your homework will make a difference in your class work.
- Jasmine, I like seeing you come to class on time.
- Jamie, you almost have it completed.
- Manuel, you are this close (teacher gestures) to finishing your assignment.

Extended Praise
- Juan, excellent, this is the best paper you have written this year in my class.
- Bill, nice job of getting your assignments in on time and putting thought into your work.
- Rose, congratulations, you really discovered another answer to the problem.
- Sarah, great job of completing your Civil War assignment, your writing is very clear and see p. 35 for ending.
- Sam, you really mastered the beginning structure of a topic sentence for your news article.
- David, much better use of first person in your writing.
- Linda, exactly, your answers show you understand and can give examples which explain the concept of gravity.

Figure 3.2. 70 Ways to Vary Your Praise

SOURCE: Freiberg (1991). © 1991 Consistency Management Associates. Used with permission.

Jose: The Periodic Table allows us to see both natural and human-made elements. It also gives information about the atomic weights and the abbreviated names for each of the elements. I was thinking, it could be useful to have a copy of the Periodic Table on the wall while we are studying this subject.

Teacher: Jose, that's a great idea!

Sarah: Yeah, perhaps each of use could be responsible for two or three elements, place them on a $8\frac{1}{2} \times 11$ piece of paper, and then we could sort them on the wall in the back of the room to form the table.

Teacher: I like the ideas of Jose and Sarah, and we could construct our Periodic Table with each student in all my classes completing one element. This way, all of the students would be part of the project. How could we create a format that would be consistent across classes and students?

The use of student ideas is a powerful motivational tool in the classroom and builds an interactive curriculum. Peterson (1992), in a study of mathematics instruction of a third grade teacher, found that "Keisha (the teacher) seems to have discovered the power of what Flanders (1970) referred to as 'use of student ideas'" (p. 172). Using student ideas gives dignity to students by integrating their ideas and knowledge into the mainstream of the classroom.

Student Feedback

Combining the self-assessment with student feedback during the same lesson will provide several sources of data about your teaching. Students have a keen sense of what teachers are doing. By 5th grade a student has seen more than 8,000 hours of instruction (180 days × 7.5 hours × 6 years). Our students have much to offer in the way of feedback. The Teacher Effectiveness Questionnaire (see Figure 3.3) provides for student feedback, beginning at the 4th grade and continuing through 12th grade. The 7-point scale has some of the adjectives reversed to minimize checking only one side. There are 16 questions; a score of 16 would be the best feedback score, with 112 being the worst feedback score. A

Teacher: _____ Expected Final Grade _____ Grade Level _____

Instructions: The following lines represent traits commonly noted by students when describing their teachers. Please place a check mark (√) on that part of the line which would indicate how you would rate your teacher. Each line should be checked.

1	2	3	4	5	6	7

Poor			Organization			Good
7	6	5	4	3	2	1
Thorough			Preparation			Unprepared
1	2	3	4	5	6	7
Limited		Subject matter knowledge				Current
1	2	3	4	5	6	7
Dull			Presentation			Interesting
7	6	5	4	3	2	1
Open minded			Attitude			Biased
1	2	3	4	5	6	7
No			Sense of humor			Yes
7	6	5	4	3	2	1
Interesting			Personality			Poor
7	6	5	4	3	2	1
Encourages			Discussion			Prohibits

Figure 3.3. Teaching Effectiveness Questionnaire
SOURCE: Freiberg (1972). Used by permission.

space at the bottom of the Teacher Effectiveness Questionnaire should be used for student comments.

Conclusion

This chapter began with the statement that knowledge is power, but knowledge about oneself is the greatest power. The

1	2	3	4	5	6	7

Boring			Speaker			Effective
7	6	5	4	3	2	1

Respects			Student			Belittles
1	2	3	4	5	6	7

Ignores			Student's needs			Recognizes
7	6	5	4	3	2	1

Clear		What is expected of student				Unclear
1	2	3	4	5	6	7

Unfair			Fairness			Fair
1	2	3	4	5	6	7

Not			Warmth			Very
7	6	5	4	3	2	1

Very			Flexible			Not
1	2	3	4	5	6	7

Not			Enthusiastic			Very

Comments:

What did you most like about this class?

Figure 3.3. Continued

process of teacher education can be enhanced through self-assessment (Freiberg & Waxman, 1990). Self-assessment requires some measures to judge accurately at a later time what has occurred in the classroom. The LISAM and TEQ may be used exclusively by yourself or shared with a cooperating teacher, university supervisor, or colleague. Once you receive the data from both instruments, ask yourself the following questions:

1. What are specific areas of strength in the lesson?
2. What are specific areas of weakness in the lesson?
3. What changes need to be made to reteach the lesson?

Reflecting on these questions, by yourself or with the assistance of others, will add greatly to your instructional repertoire. The self-assessment process will also facilitate your move along the pathway from novice to expert teacher.

Note

1. This section is derived from the original descriptions of the LISAM instrument (Freiberg, 1987).

References

Anderson, J. B., & Freiberg, H. J. (in press). Using self-assessment as a reflective tool to enhance the student teaching experience. *Teacher Education Quarterly.*

Bailey, G. D. (1981). *Teacher self-assessment: A means for improving classroom instruction.* Washington, DC: National Education Association.

Brophy J. E., & Good, T. L. (1986). Teacher behavior and student achievement. In M. C. Wittrock (Ed.), *Handbook of research on teaching* (3rd ed.). New York: Macmillan.

Cameron, J., & Pierce, W. D. (1994). Reinforcement, reward, and intrinsic motivation: A meta-analysis. *Review of Educational Research, 64,* 363-423.

Carlsen, W. S. (1991). Questioning in classrooms: A sociolinguistic perspective. *Review of Educational Research, 61,* 157-178.

Evertson, C. M., & Burry, J. T. (1989). Capturing classroom context: The observation system as lens for assessment. *Journal of Personnel Evaluation in Education, 2,* 297-320.

Flanders, N. (1970). *Analyzing classroom behavior.* New York: Addison-Wesley.

Freiberg, H. J. (1972). *An investigation of similar and different ability groups in secondary classrooms.* Amherst: University of Massachusetts.

Freiberg, H. J. (1987). Teacher self-assessment and principal supervision. *NASSP Bulletin, 71*(498), 85-92.

Freiberg, H. J. (1991). *Consistency management: What to do the first days and weeks of school* (Training booklet). Houston, Texas.

Freiberg, H. J., & Driscoll, A. (1992). *Universal teaching strategies.* Boston: Allyn & Bacon.

Freiberg, H. J., & Driscoll, A. (in press). *Universal teaching strategies* (2nd ed.). Boston: Allyn & Bacon.

Freiberg, H. J., & Waxman, H. C. (1988). Alternative feedback approaches for improving student teachers' classroom instruction. *Journal of Teacher Education, 39*(4), 8-14.

Freiberg, H. J., & Waxman, H. C. (1990). Changing teacher education. In W. R. Houston (Ed.), *Handbook of research on teacher education.* New York: Macmillan.

Freiberg, H. J., Waxman, H. C., & Houston, W. R. (1987). Enriching feedback to student teachers through small group discussion. *Teacher Education Quarterly, 14*(3), 71-82.

Good T. L., & Brophy, J. E. (1994). *Looking in classrooms* (6th ed.). New York: HarperCollins.

Guyton, E., & McIntyre, D. J. (1990). Student teaching and school experiences. In W. R. Houston (Ed.), *Handbook of research on teacher education.* New York: Macmillan.

Harris, A. H. (1988). *Sources of treatment effects in a teacher effectiveness training program.* Doctoral dissertation, Vanderbilt University.

Hook, C., & Rosenshine, B. (1979). Accuracy of teacher reports of their classroom behavior. *Review of Educational Research, 49,* 1-12.

Kerry, T. (1987). Classroom questions in England. *Questioning Exchange, 1*(1), 33.

Kremer-Hayon, L. (1993). *Teacher self-evaluation: Teachers in their own mirrors.* Boston: Kluwer.

Peterson, P. L. (1992). Revising their thinking: Keisha Coleman and her third-grade mathematics class. In H. H. Marshall (Ed.), *Redefining student learning.* Norwood, NJ: Ablex.

Rogers, C. R., & Freiberg, H. J. (1994). *Freedom to learn* (3rd ed.). Columbus, OH: Merrill/Macmillan.

Rowe, M. B. (1969). Science, soul and sanctions. *Science and Children, 6*(6), 11-13.

Rowe, M. B. (1974). Wait time and rewards as instructional variables, their influence in language, logic and fate control: Part one—Wait time. *Journal of Research in Science Teaching, 11*(2), 81-94.

Schuck, R. F. (1985). An empirical analysis of the power of set induction and systematic questioning as instructional strategies. *Journal of Teacher Education, 36*(2), 38-43.

Stallings, J., & Freiberg, H. J. (1991). Observation for the improvement of teaching. In H. Waxman & H. Walberg (Eds.), *Effective teaching: Current research* (pp. 107-133). Berkeley, CA: McCutchan.

Stallings, J. A., Martin, A., & Bossung, J. (in press). Houston teaching academy: A partnership in developing teachers. *Teaching and Teacher Education*.

Wragg, E. C. (1993). *Primary teaching skills*. London: Routledge.

❖ 4 ❖

A Legal Primer
for Student Teachers

JULIE FISHER MEAD
JULIE K. UNDERWOOD

As college students enter their first field experience, they slowly begin to learn what it truly means to be a professional educator, accepting the mantle of responsibility for children. That mantle is a complex one, composed of professional competence, artistic implementation, judgment, and caring. Another aspect of that mantle involves the legal rights and responsibilities of being a teacher. Issues of liability when a child is hurt probably spring to mind first. In addition, student records, academic freedom, and due process rights for teachers are legal issues that should be understood by those entering the classroom for the first time.

This chapter focuses on just these issues. What follows are four questions commonly asked by preservice teachers and responses to those questions. Although not all-encompassing, these four topics—negligence, student records, academic freedom, and due process—form an introduction to some of the legal issues involved in teaching. The chapter closes with some advice for student teachers and those who supervise and instruct them.

Negligence: When Am I Liable if a Child Is Hurt While I'm in Charge?

Liability is an issue of negligence, and negligence is a civil wrong or tort. Claims of negligence are filed in civil court and, if successful, result in awards of damages sustained. Negligence occurs when one person owes a duty to another and breaches that duty, resulting in an injury.

To sustain a claim of negligence, the court considers the following four questions. Each one forms a component of negligence and *all* must be answered *affirmatively* for negligence to be found.

1. Did the teacher or student teacher owe a *duty* to protect others from reasonable risk?
2. Was that duty *breached*?
3. Was the breach of duty the *proximate cause* of the injury?
4. Was someone actually *injured*?

The nature of compulsory schooling creates a special relationship between students and teachers. In essence, the school staff act in place of the parents while children are in their care. This concept, called the doctrine of *in loco parentis,* suggests the school's duty to protect children from injuries (e.g., supervise, provide safety instructions, warn of potential dangers, maintain safe equipment and facilities). As one might surmise, that duty changes, depending on the age and abilities of the children and the type and location of the activity. Older children are expected to predict the consequences of their actions to a greater degree than younger children. For example, teachers owe a greater duty to 1st graders than to 12th graders. That duty may also be heightened by the nature of the activity. The tumbling unit in physical education class creates a greater duty for the instructors than does the Macbeth unit in English literature class.

When student teachers begin their assignments, they too assume that duty to protect. In addition, the presence of a student teacher creates some extra duties for the cooperating teacher and the university supervisor. In essence, both of these parties, as part of their duty to protect the minor children in the class, have the obligation to be certain that the student teacher is adequately trained to handle the activity before transferring the class to the beginning teacher's care.

The second component of negligence is breach of duty. To determine whether someone has breached his or her duty, the court compares his or her actions with that of the "reasonable person." In other words, would a reasonable person, with the same knowledge, skills, and abilities, have behaved in a similar manner in the same situation? Would a reasonable person have foreseen that acting (or failing to act) could bring harm to someone? If the court concludes either that the person behaved reasonably, given the circumstances, or that the injury that ensued could not have been foreseen, no breach of duty will be found. Without a breach of duty, no negligence can be concluded.

If the court finds that a person accused of negligence owed a duty and breached that duty, then it will consider whether the breach of duty was the proximate cause of the injury suffered. Or stated another way, did the person's acts or failure to act cause the injury? Were there any intervening acts between the time of the breach and the onset of injury? Was the injury, in fact, simply an accident? Again, unless it can be shown that a breach of duty actually caused the injury, a claim of negligence cannot be supported.

So, when is a student teacher liable if a child is hurt while he or she is in charge? When the student teacher acts in an unreasonable manner that directly results in the child's injuries. Therefore, the prudent student teacher is cognizant of his or her duties to protect the children in the class and seeks the guidance and support of the cooperating teacher and university supervisor to prepare him or her to fulfill those duties.

Student Records: Is It Appropriate
for Me to Look at Student Records?

Student records are protected by the Family Educational Rights and Privacy Act (FERPA) (20 U.S.C.A. §1232G). This act guarantees parental access to student records and restricts the school's use and dissemination of them. In essence, records access is restricted to persons within the school system and state and federal governments that have "legitimate educational interests" in the information contained within a student's file. Express parental permission is required before the records may be made available to anyone else.

Student teachers have that "legitimate educational interest" for at least two reasons. First, the information contained in the files may help them to better instruct the children in their care. Second, they may in fact be adding to those files by entering students' grades and discipline reports. Therefore, student teachers may have access to student records for professional purposes.

However, cooperating teachers and university supervisors should ensure that student teachers understand the proper use of those records and the restrictions placed upon their use under FERPA. Only when student teachers understand their obligation to keep the information contained within the records in strictest confidence should those records be made available to them.

Academic Freedom: I Have a
Constitutional Right to Academic Freedom. Right?

Wrong. No explicit right to academic freedom exists. However, teachers do have a constitutional right to free speech and expression that is not "checked at the school house gate" (*Tinker v. Des Moines Independent Community School District*, 393 U.S. 503, at 506 [1969]). In addition, the U.S. Supreme Court has consistently held that the classroom ought to be a free "marketplace of ideas" (*Keyishian v. Board of Regents*, 385 U.S. 589, at 603 [1967]) and that teachers have an integral role in the dissemination of ideas.

In practice, those rights may be tempered by the curriculum. Local school districts have the authority to set and regulate the curriculum their schools deliver. Teachers of that district must abide by those policies or face the consequences of reprimand or even dismissal. Similarly, student teachers are bound by the same guidelines. For the period of time they are present in the school, they are expected to follow all of the requirements and prohibitions enacted by the district through its curriculum. This may include specific methodologies, textbooks, books, magazines, or movies to use or refrain from using.

In addition, in recognition of the captive audience a classroom of students represents, and the impressionable minds of those children, courts have upheld disciplinary actions against teachers who choose materials which may not be specifically prohibited, but which the court believes the teacher should have known were inappropriate. For example, a Kentucky teacher was discharged for showing the "R" rated movie, *Pink Floyd—The Wall* to her high school students on the last day of school (*Fowler v. Board of Education of Lincoln County*, 819 F. 2d 657 [6th Cir. 1987]).

By the same token, if a court concludes that a teacher had no way of knowing that actions would be improper, the teacher cannot be dismissed for them. In *Moore v. Gaston County Board of Education*, 357 F. Supp. 1037 (W.D.N.C. 1973), a court ruled in favor of a student teacher who challenged the discharge from his student teaching assignment. School authorities terminated his student teaching assignment because he responded to the questions of students by indicating his personal religious beliefs and a belief in Darwinian theory during a history lesson related to a textbook chapter titled "The Middle East—A Flowering of Religion." In this case, the court reasoned:

> No instructions, specific or general, had been given to the plaintiff with regard to how he should teach the particular lesson nor as to whether he should answer or evade honest questions from the children. . . . Our laws in this country have long recognized that no person should be punished for conduct unless such conduct has been proscribed in clear and precise terms. (pp. 1039-1040)

However, the court also included the following caveat:

It is not called for, on this record, to speculate what restriction on honest inquiry might have been allowable if school authorities had given clear notice to the teacher. (p. 1044)

A prudent student teacher would discuss all materials and lesson plans with the cooperating teacher in order to avoid incidents based upon lesson content. Although perhaps disheartening, student teachers must learn that in the K-12 system, academic freedom is extremely limited.

Due Process Rights: What Are My Rights if Things Are Not Going Well?

Student teachers, as do all students, have a constitutional interest in being treated fairly. The Fourteenth Amendment protects against the deprivation of life, liberty, and property without due process. Courts have consistently found that students have liberty and property interests in their education, especially at this level. Those interests cannot be abridged without good reason and appropriate due process.

The right to due process comprises two components. The first, substantive due process, is an issue of basic fairness. The state, or in this case, public schools and universities, must have a valid reason for the actions they take with regard to a student teacher's performance. In addition, the means must be reasonably calculated to achieve those ends. Courts recognize a college or university's interest in protecting the reputation of its diploma and ensuring that its graduates are in fact ready to teach. However, the rules employed must be reasonable and related to the goal of the preparation of teachers.

In the case of a student teacher who is doing poorly, the court would look to see whether the problems were clearly explained to the student. They would also examine whether the problems were remediable and, if so, whether adequate time and instruction had been given for the student teacher to improve. For example, a student teacher's drug use might be considered beyond remedy (See *Lai v. Board of Trustees of East Carolina University*, 330 F. Supp. 904 [E.D.N.C. 1971]).

The second component of due process is that of procedural due process. Procedures must be in place to ensure the accuracy of the determination. In the case of dismissal of a student teacher from the teacher education program, that due process would be expected to include notice of the problem motivating the dismissal, an opportunity for the student to present his or her side of the issue, a hearing before some impartial party, and a decision based upon the facts gathered.

When such process has been provided, and the actions of the university have been reasonably related to producing qualified teachers, courts have upheld the dismissals (See *Lai v. Board of Trustees of East Carolina University*, 330 F. Supp. 904 [E.D.N.C. 1971]). When such process has been denied, the student teacher has prevailed (See *Moore v. Gaston County Board of Education*, 357 F. Supp. 1037 [W.D.N.C. 1973]). In addition, courts will refuse to hear cases if students have not completed the grievance procedures available at the university (See *Hoffman v. Grove*, 171 S.E. 2d 810 [W. Va. 1983]).

One final issue of due process must be understood. The basis for the above requirements presupposes the presence of a "state actor"; in other words, some person or institution connected to government. Students of private colleges and universities cannot challenge negative actions under the Fourteenth Amendment right to due process, because there is no state actor (See *Rowe v. Chandler*, 332 F. Supp. 336 [D. Ks. 1971]). Students in such a predicament may be able to challenge the college's actions under other theories of law (e.g., contract law) but do not have the same avenues for challenge as do their peers at public institutions.

Some Suggestions

The best way to prevent legal problems is to be informed. The following suggestions provide a means to begin that process of information.

1. Read the teacher's handbook, if one is available, and discuss its contents with the cooperating teacher. Be sure you understand its requirements and its prohibitions. Cooperating teachers

and university supervisors should consider this task an important introduction to becoming a teacher.

2. Thoroughly discuss school safety rules and regulations. Be certain you know what to do in case of emergency, before assuming complete control of the classroom.

3. Be aware of the potential hazards associated with any activity and act accordingly to protect children from those dangers.

4. Be certain you know what controls the district has placed on the curriculum you will be teaching. Are there specific texts and/or methodologies that district policy requires or prohibits?

5. Be certain that student records are used to enhance and inform your teaching. Make certain that strict confidentiality is respected.

6. Document any problems you have with students, or as a student teacher, in case you are called upon to relate details at a later time.

7. University supervisors should carefully review with the student teacher the procedures in place for a student who wishes to challenge the grade given for student teaching. Likewise, the types of acts for which the university would institute dismissal from the teacher education program and the procedures employed to effect such a dismissal should be made known to the student teacher at the onset of the assignment. Colleges and universities with no policies in place should create them.

8. Both cooperating teachers and university supervisors should maintain detailed notes of the student teacher's progress, including conversations with the student teacher about his or her performance, in order to substantiate the grade given or other actions taken.

9. Take a school law class. It would be a mistake to conclude that the topics covered in this chapter are the only issues confront-

ing today's teachers. On the contrary, teachers of today must have a broader and firmer understanding of a wide range of legal issues. For example, space does not allow discussion of the following issues of school law:

— certification
— child abuse
— curricular control
— discrimination
— separation of church and state
— special education
— student discipline
— student freedoms
— teacher contracts
— teacher dismissal
— teacher freedoms

In summary, the evolution of the student teacher into the professional educator is a multifaceted process. Understanding the legal aspects of the teaching profession forms one of those facets. Issues of negligence, student records, academic freedom, and due process for teachers represent only a fraction of the topics that can be viewed from a legal perspective. By fully comprehending the legal rights and responsibilities of teachers and students, student teachers can better become not simply dispensers of information but truly professional educators.

Recommended Reading

Camp, W., Underwood, J., Connelly, M., & Lane, K. (1993). *Principal's legal handbook*. Topeka, KS: National Organization for Legal Problems in Education.

McCarthy, M., & Cambron-McCabe, N. (1992). *Public school law: Teachers' and students' rights*. Needham Heights, MA: Allyn & Bacon.

❖ 5 ❖

Field Experiences in Multicultural Environments

RAFAEL LARA-ALECIO
EMILIO RENDON

The field experiences of student teaching can be a time of great joy, expectation, trepidation, and fear. As a student teacher, you begin your voyage into a new career where you are often excited to work directly with a classroom of children, who in past field experiences simply have been observed from a distance or worked with minimally. There is an excitement in your face, but there is perhaps a fearful voice within saying: "Who are these students? Can I do this? Can I teach these students so that they will learn? Can I get along well in this school and with my supervising teacher?" The answers to these questions often lie in how you perceive your world.

This chapter will explore a view of the world that is very important in responding to the questions and fears student teachers often face in their field experience. It will explore the multicultural environment, issues surrounding the multicultural view, and six effective strategies student teachers can use in their classrooms.

The Multicultural Environment Defined

The world that we view through our eyes is changing rapidly, and these rapid changes are reflected in the demographics of our classrooms. When we look into a classroom today, we see a mosaic of ethnic groups that currently make up the population of the United States. By the year 2020, the United States will be a country of minorities, thus reflected in our school population. In some states, such as Texas, this is already true, with more than 50% of the school population classified as minority. But a multicultural environment is more than just looking at ethnic diversity within a classroom.

The multicultural environment involves an ongoing process that is facilitated by the teacher in the classroom. It is an environment where there are sensitivity, awareness, respect, understanding, and acceptance of differing cultures and languages. It is one in which the varied cultures develop a rich source of learning as topics are covered in class through local, state, national, and international perspectives. The environment is not only sensitive to ethnic cultural differences but also reminiscent of other types of cultural diversity found among languages, genders, exceptionalities (special needs students), socioeconomic levels, religions, or localities (rural, urban). In the multicultural environment worth and significance are given to similarities and differences between and among individuals within the various cultural groups.

Consciousness of a multicultural environment is the first step you can take in the process of developing positive perceptions of this type of environment. When you are aware of the various cultures within your classroom, then greater sensitivity will be practiced as your lessons are developed and taught.

Some Considerations
in the Multicultural Environment

As student teachers, it is important that you realize that this sensitivity to the multicultural environment will not occur immediately. It is not an end in itself; rather it is an ongoing, lifelong process of exploration, research, dialogue, self-analysis, sensitivity, respect, and awareness. In this case, more is better, and the more you engage yourself in learning about and talking with people of other cultures, the more you will begin to develop your multicultural environment. If you fail to attend to cultural diversity in the arenas of human activity, you may find yourself perpetuating a world that is less than accepting, a world in which many people are treated as less equal than others. In the classroom, this act would be paradoxical to learning and to the development of self-esteem in students.

Effective Strategies in the
Development of the Multicultural Environment

The major strategy in the development of a multicultural environment is to attune yourself to becoming a critical thinker along with your students. You must think seriously and critically about local, state, national, and international issues. When you begin to think critically, you can better facilitate and promote this thought process in your students.

The first step in working in or developing a multicultural environment is to look within. You must first know your own culture—who you are, where you come from, how you feel about your own culture. Remember, your culture may be multilayered in that you may be African American, female, of middle-class socioeconomic status, suburban, and Christian. Your worldview will be seen through those lenses. You will need to make sure you have those lenses focused sharply.

The second step will be to clarify your own values, attitudes, beliefs, and even prejudices with regard to individuals in cultural groups different from your own. For example, ask yourself: "How do I feel about the (Hispanic American, African American, Native American, Jewish, etc.) ethnic group? How do I feel about having a physically challenged student in my classroom, and how will I facilitate his or her learning? How do I feel about students who differ in their religious beliefs, and can I work with their parents without offending them? How often do I call upon differing genders in the classroom to answer math, science, or language arts questions?" This is one way in which you can begin to clarify how you feel about various cultural groups.

The third step is to increase your information base about various cultures through reading, talking with people from differing backgrounds, traveling to other parts of the country and the world, visiting a church service of another culture, cooking and eating a dish from another culture, visiting a rural school, evaluating books for ethnic or gender bias, joining and supporting a minority organization in town, or watching documentaries. You will want to pay careful attention to the particular culture's customs and beliefs. For example, did you know that (generally) the Hispanic culture is very much group oriented? They do not tend to like competition, rather they thrive in cooperative situations. However, this should not disallow Hispanic students from choosing leadership roles within your classroom or from choosing independent study work. This could have an impact on how you would structure activities for the Hispanic students in your classroom. This is but one example of building your information base and using it constructively in your classroom. A reminder: There are certain stereotypes you may find in the literature of specific cultures that may cause information bias and not the positive building of your information base. You must remain open-minded and think critically so that you can absorb what is similar and what is different to your own culture in order to be able to respect such differences.

The fourth step is to read about or take course work in working with differing cultures. A course such as Methods for Teaching Exceptional Children, English as a Second Language for International and Intercultural Settings, or Methods/Approaches for Teaching English as a Second Language would be helpful. The more strategies you have in your repertoire of knowledge, the more confident and effective you will feel in your multicultural classroom. Other methods that would be applicable in a multicultural environment would make use of learning styles, communication styles, cooperative learning, and integrated instruction.

Learning styles research is well documented in the field of cultural diversity (Nieto, 1992). Learning styles are important to consider in the multicultural environment, because research indicates that various cultural groups have differing learning styles that would affect instruction. There are many ways to assess learning styles for the purpose of choosing appropriate instructional strategies. Your supervising teacher, your professor, or your principal may be sources of information on this type of assessment and its appropriate uses within the classroom.

Communication styles among various ethnic groups and cultures have also been documented (Nieto, 1992). Clear communication with students and with parents is necessary for student achievement. Williams (1981) found that urban African American students were often perceived by their teachers as misbehaving and intimidating. A savvy teacher would use this communicative information to his or her advantage. A prime example can be viewed in the movie *Stand and Deliver*, in which Jaime Escalante uses drama and shock in his classroom as a means of communicating with his minority students. Teachers need to be sensitive to different cultural communication customs. For example, it is not disrespectful for a Hispanic child or an Asian child not to look the adult in the eye when being corrected; rather, it is an act of respect. Sensitivity and awareness of such cultural communication patterns are essential in building a multicultural environment and understanding.

Cooperative learning is a method that can be explored in a multicultural environment. Effective cooperative learning seeks to highlight how different cultural groups can accomplish more by working together. It tends to emphasize a learning community, which suggests that all are worthy and have something to contribute. Without the contribution of all students' individual participation, the spirit of the multicultural cooperative environment would be lacking. A variety of culturally sensitive vocabulary words can be used in the cooperative groups within the classroom.

For example, in developing social skills in the cooperative groups, there are many ways to say "good job" in many different languages. These can be listed and used by the teacher and the students in the classroom groups. Cooperative learning emphasizes interdependence, rather than independence or dependence, and builds important social skills necessary for success in our global world.

An integrated curriculum assists the development of a multicultural environment. Since multiculturalism embraces many disciplines, such as anthropology, social studies, psychology, physical science, mathematics, law, religion, music, art, languages, architecture, and political science, development of thematic units that integrate the disciplines would be appropriate. Additionally, as you integrate the disciplines, you will want to include cultural literature and visuals depicting the various cultures. When developing problems for your students, use culturally representative names within your text or stories. When developing thematic units, try to include a resource person from the community who can share various cultural traditions. For example, if you are studying textiles and trade, you may have an Italian merchant in town who can share typical fabrics from Italy as well as how trade is handled in that country. The integration of the curriculum would assist in viewing the world from a holistic rather than a separate vantage point.

A fifth step in the development of a multicultural environment is to practice inclusion within your classroom. Model for your students acceptance of all students, regardless of their backgrounds, language, learning curve, or dress. This also implies the setting of high expectations for all students and motivating students to learn. This is done in part by establishing a respectful, caring, risk-free environment. Know your students and their families as individuals and include the parents in the education of their children.

A sixth step is to assess yourself in the classroom. How are you responding to the various cultural groups within the classroom? In order to assess this, you may have to ask your supervising teacher or professor to observe you for this specific reason. You may wish to videotape a lesson and review it for any cultural biases. How many times do you call on your exceptional students in your class? How many times do you call on girls/boys? How many times do you positively reinforce that "you as a girl" can solve this math problem correctly? How many times do you call on your language diverse students? These are the types of questions you may place in an observation matrix for yourself or an outside observer.

A final, but important, step is to assess and evaluate your practices within your classroom for superficiality. Check to see that your practice goes beyond simply pronouncing a few ethnic words, wearing a costume, eating a certain food, letting a girl do a science project, observing Kwanza, Hanukkah, Black History Month, and Cinco de Mayo, or simply remembering Native Americans on Thanksgiving Day. The multicultural environment is one that is a continuous, integrated curricular experience, not one that is disjointed and fragmented. The experiences should be ongoing, conceptual, core activities that may be obtrusive or unobtrusive in nature.

Summary

The student teacher and the student of field experiences will most likely find himself or herself in a multicultural setting. Making the most of this setting and turning it into an effective multicultural environment is truly up to the individual and is an ongoing process, not a one-time event. One thing is certain: The time has long passed when we can, or should, be all of one generic identity. There is nothing wrong or improper about varied people wanting to take pride in their particular identities and feel worthwhile at whatever their station in life. The words of the late Robert Kennedy on June 21, 1968, apply. He said, " . . . discrimination is not worthy of us. . . . The stifling air of prejudice is not fit to be breathed by . . . a nation that . . . calls itself free . . . " (Dineen, 1968).

You, as the student teacher or student of field experiences, are in a prime position to take a proactive stance for building sensitivity for the multicultural environments that exist in today's society. Seven steps toward that structure have been suggested in this chapter. It is up to you to determine to take the first step to embracing an inclusive, multicultural classroom environment.

References

Dineen, M. P. (Ed.). (1968). *America the Beautiful in the words of Robert F. Kennedy*. New York: G. P. Putnam.

Nieto, S. (1992). *Affirming diversity*. New York: Longman.

Williams, M. D. (1981). Observations in Pittsburgh ghetto schools. *Anthropology and Education Quarterly, 12*, 211-220.

❖ 6 ❖

Using Technology
to Prepare Teachers

Future Possibilities

JOAN P. SEBASTIAN

It was Friday of the third week of student teaching and Susan was exhausted. She drove to her home, musing over the hectic week in the third grade classroom. Had she done anything right, had anyone learned anything this week? Dropping her briefcase as she walked through the door, Susan went straight to the computer and logged on to the E-mail system. She typed one word, "HELP," and sent the message to 15 other student teachers in her cohort.

Susan will access resources (ideas/suggestions/materials) and emotional support to help her plan for Monday morning. Rather than waiting until the next student teaching seminar, or attempting to catch up with some of her peers on the phone, by the end of the weekend she will have received E-mail messages from several of the student teachers. This dialogue among the student teachers connected by E-mail will provide almost immediate support and assistance for all of them through an "electronic community" of learners.

In an isolated rural community, a small group of teacher certification candidates sits around a television screen, participating in a graduate special education certification course. The instructor teaching the class is on a university campus 200 miles away. The cohort of distance students is presenting a group report on issues in rural schools. Each week this cohort and two other cohorts at equally remote sites meet, via live interactive television, with the campus methods class. These students will complete a graduate certification program without leaving their rural communities.

Five student teachers gather closely around a computer screen as they work through information for a case study assignment. The computer program provides them with multiple kinds of data to consider: test scores, student work samples, interviews, and video clips of the case student's classroom behavior. The student teachers work as a team to develop an instructional program to address the problems presented by the case.

Each of these scenarios illustrates how technology is used currently in the preparation of teachers. Preparing teachers through the use of new technologies is full of promise and frustration for everyone involved. The learning curve is steep. As teacher educators, we need to learn new uses for both familiar and new technologies, and then apply that knowledge to our practice. This chapter will explore some of the unique possibilities offered by technology for the preparation of teachers. Along with these possibilities, some cautions and possible outcomes will be identified. In the final analysis, we have nothing to lose (some time and energy, maybe) and much to gain by learning new ways to do our work.

What Are the Possibilities?

It seems that every few months a new computer or a must-have application appears on the market. Keeping up with the rapid growth of the telecommunications industry is impossible, and the right time to get involved never really comes. At some point, we just have to jump in and give it a try.

Several different kinds of technological applications have potential for use in teacher education programs. Three example applications, (1) telecommunications/distance education approaches, (2) computer-designed instructional programs, and (3) computer-mediated communications systems, along with the possibilities they offer, are briefly described in the following sections.

Telecommunications/Distance Education Approaches

Distance education occurs when the learner is separated from the instructor by space or time. Traditional print-based distance learning (correspondence study) has expanded to include telecommunications technologies, which offer a range of interactive capabilities to facilitate communication between and among learners and instructors.

Participating in education and training programs at a distance, through the use of a variety of telecommunications technologies, is growing more and more common (Moore, Thompson, et al., 1990). These technologies offer access to learning opportunities for individuals who, because of travel distances and other life circumstances, would otherwise be unable to obtain the information. Approaches to the delivery of instruction at a distance include such technologies as one-way and two-way audio and video, satellite, prerecorded videotaped instruction, computer systems, narrowcast cable television, telephones, and radio and television broadcasts.

A simple and cost-effective distance teacher education application is the use of telephone bridges or conference calling systems. Course readings and assignments are supported by weekly lectures and discussions held over the phone lines to multiple rural communities. Commercial and locally produced videotapes add a visual component to audio-based programs. Campus instructors often travel to remote locations to supervise student teachers in rural classroom settings (Royce, Cummings, & Cheney, 1989).

More recently, distance education approaches have been effectively supplemented with a variety of television/video technologies (Egan, McCleary, Sebastian, & Lacy, 1988). Live two-way audio and video systems (satellite and microwave broadcast systems) provide enhanced communication opportunities for distance students. The visual and audio information expands the kinds of learning experiences distance students are able to share with campus classrooms. Additionally, holding weekly seminars over an interactive television system facilitates communication among student teachers and supervisors, and it eliminates the need for additional trips to the distance site.

Prerecorded videotaped courses and training modules are also used to deliver information and instruction to teacher candidates at a distance. Students, working with a cohort or independently, view the videotapes as if they were attending a conventional campus-based course. Study groups, supported by on-site distance education facilitators, come together to discuss content and work in cooperative learning groups. The course instructor is available via phone or interactive television. Feedback on assignments and activities, critical for student growth, is provided quickly by facsimile (fax) and E-mail systems. Additional support and mentoring for student teachers is provided by the on-site distance facilitators who are also master classroom teachers.

Most distance education systems use an integrated approach for delivering instruction to students at a distance. By capitalizing on the technologies that are available, and attending to the learning needs of students, these model programs are able to help remote communities address a critical shortage of qualified educational personnel (Brush, Knapczyk, & Hubbard, 1994; Sebastian, 1990). Additionally, by combining technologies the added costs for distance delivery can be more efficiently managed.

Computer-Designed Instruction

In the past 10 years, user-friendly computer technology has become available to the general public, yet computer use for purposes other than word processing, data management, and statistical analysis in higher education is in its infancy. Basic computer literacy courses are available and often required in many teacher preparation programs. Colleges of education around the country are exploring other potential applications for computer use in the preparation of teachers (Bright, 1993; Esplin, 1994; Waugh, 1993).

Recent advances in interactive multimedia computer applications have provided teacher educators with the means for developing technology-enhanced class presentations. Lecture outlines and course content can be integrated with audio, video, film, and slides to illustrate learning models and instructional methods. Using multimedia applications, instructors can develop presentations that will provide teacher trainees with example classroom contexts in which to apply their learning.

Computer applications of the case method approach used in many teacher education programs are also under development. Case examples, which are often in narrative form, can be created by using integrated media programs. The mediated case example may include sample documents, audio interviews, video clips of classroom activity, and the like to provide a more realistic and interactive environment for student teachers. Working in teams or cooperative learning groups, student teachers can solve problems in "virtual" educational settings (Merideth & Lotfipour, 1993; Reilly, Hull, & Greenleaf, 1993).

Adding a degree of reality to pedagogical instruction through computer-mediated learning activities provides teacher trainees with a window into the classroom. Activities such as these can help to prepare students for future field experiences, because they learn to reflect on small samples of real classroom experiences.

Computer-Mediated Communications

A third application of new technology that holds much promise for the preparation of teachers, particularly during field experiences, is the use of computer-mediated communication systems. These systems, more commonly known as E-mail and computer conferencing, provide innovative ways for student teachers and field supervisors to communicate about the field experience.

The importance of developing in novice teachers the ability to reflect on their practice of teaching has been well established (Posner, 1989). Requiring journal entries during field experiences is a common strategy used by teacher educators to help student teachers learn to reflect on their beginning teaching experience. Often, there is a delay between the time the journal entry is made and when the supervisor is able to respond to the student. E-mail journal entries can be used to facilitate a more immediate interaction between student teachers and their supervisors (Thompson & Hayes, 1993).

Student teachers, when provided access to a computer with a communications program and modem, can send their daily journal reflections directly to the supervisor. Field supervisors are able to respond to these reflections quickly, providing thought-provoking suggestions and comments. The immediacy of the interaction facilitates the student's growth during the field experience and, it is hoped, develops the student's ability to think critically about his or her teaching.

Computer conferencing is another communications application with promise for use during field experiences. Computer conferencing, the combination of word processing and telecommunication via personal computers, telephone lines, and central computer conferencing systems, offers creative possibilities for developing interaction among individuals (Levinson, 1990).

Using a computer conferencing system to connect student teachers to one another and their supervisors can alleviate the sense of isolation student teachers often experience in field settings. Initially, the dialogue that occurs over the computer conference provides support and may alleviate frustration for student teachers. It helps students to know that their peers are also struggling with basic classroom management those first few weeks of the field experience. Later, student teachers are able to share content-specific ideas and strategies with one another as they attempt to address curriculum issues and individual student needs (Hoover, 1994).

Finally, networking via computers connects individuals around the world. Locating and exchanging information from worldwide sources is now possible. Student teachers can tap into international networks to access all kinds of information and resources. Using E-mail network bulletin boards, student teachers can find job openings in areas where they may want to locate, as well as interact with other educators worldwide who may have similar content interests.

What Are the Challenges?

Technology, though providing new and creative possibilities for teacher preparation, also presents us with several challenges. Two issues that are often viewed as barriers to implementation are (1) access to new technologies and (2) knowledge and skill in the use of different technological applications.

Before we can begin to explore the many possibilities offered by technology in the preparation of teachers, instructors must first have access to the hardware (computers and telecommunications systems) and software (applications and programs). Most institutions of higher education provide faculty with some kind of computer access, but in order to use many of the newer applications, computers and the corresponding software must be updated frequently. Students as well as faculty must have ready access to computers if networking during field experiences is to be useful.

Another challenge, in the application of technology in teacher education, is the need for personnel who can support faculty in their use of the technology. Without technical support, instructors are often unable to maximize the creative options offered by a technology. In addition to access and technical support, instructors need training in the use of new technological systems. For example, teaching on television presents unique challenges and requires that instructors use different strategies for presenting information and involving students (Egan, Ferraris, Jones, & Sebastian, 1993; Egan, Sebastian, Welch, & Page, 1993). Many distance education programs require that instructors complete a training program that includes practice in front of a television camera. Additionally, telecourse instructors often work with an instructional design team that provides further support and coaching.

Most interactive multimedia computer applications that involve integrating video, audio, and other visual media require some kind of training prior to successful implementation. Once computer communications systems are in place, ongoing technical assistance is critical to keep systems functioning and to resolve the inevitable problems.

Technical support and training in the development and use of new technological applications are critical if the possibilities described above are to become realities. The challenge then is to ensure that teacher educators and student teachers not only have access to the technology but also receive adequate training and technical assistance. When these challenges are not addressed, the frustration that develops may interfere with the successful application of new technologies in teacher education.

What Are the Benefits?

Using technology in the preparation of teachers results in benefits for both teacher educators and student teachers. Not only can the immediate learning experience for students be enhanced, but the knowledge and skill acquired in the development of programs also have an impact on everyone involved.

Mastering a new skill, whether it is teaching on television or using a multimedia program in a class presentation, is empowering for instructors. Instructors who use technology report that their overall teaching has improved because of the creative application of a new innovation. Instructors also report a growing comfort level with technology, the more opportunity they have to experiment with its use (Egan, Sebastian, Welch, Page, Nkabinde, & Jones, 1993).

The benefits for student teachers also extend beyond their actual experience with the technology. Students who see faculty using multimedia computer applications may recognize the possibilities for their own teaching. Student teachers who learn to network over an E-mail system with colleagues during student teaching will be able to establish continuing dialogues with educators as they move into the field. By experiencing the possibilities offered by technology, future teachers will acquire the knowledge and expertise needed to infuse their teaching practice with these and future applications.

The future promise of technology in the preparation of teachers is a reality today. Only by experimenting with the many different applications of technology will we learn new ways to prepare tomorrow's teachers. The possibilities and challenges combine to create new learning opportunities for everyone involved.

References

Bright, L. (1993). South Dakota keys professional development center to technology. *The Holmes Group Forum, 7*(3), 14-16.

Brush, T., Knapczyk, D., & Hubbard, L. (1994). Incorporating technology in the field-based preparation of teachers. *Journal of Technology and Teacher Education, 2*(1), 91-102.

Egan, M. W., Ferraris, C., Jones, D. E., & Sebastian, J. (1993). The telecourse experience: A student perspective. *ed journal, 7*(5), J-1-7.

Egan, M. W., McCleary, I. D., Sebastian, J., & Lacy, H. (1988). Rural preservice teacher preparation using two-way interactive television. *Rural Special Education Quarterly, 9*(3), 27-33.

Egan, M. W., Sebastian, J., Welch, M., & Page, B. (1993). Identifying performance improvement prescriptions for distance learning and teaching: Quantitative and qualitative approaches. Distance education symposium: Selected papers part 3. *American Center for the Study of Distance Education Research Monograph No. 9,* 25-36. University Park: The Pennsylvania State University.

Egan, M. W., Sebastian, J., Welch, M., Page, B., Nkabinde, Z., & Jones, D. (1993). Quality television instruction: Perceptions of instructors. *ed journal, 7*(7), J-1-8.

Esplin, F. (1994). Going the distance: U of U is applying technological outreach as the wave of the future. *Continuum, 4*(1), 24-29.

Hoover, L. A. (1994). Use of telecomputing to support group-oriented inquiry during student teaching. *Technology and Teacher*

Education Annual. Proceedings of the Fifth Annual Conference of the Society for Technology and Teacher Education (pp. 652-655). Charlottesville, VA: The Association for the Advancement of Computing in Education.

Levinson, P. (1990). Computer conferencing in the context of the evolution of media. In L. M. Harasim (Ed.), *Online education perspectives on a new environment*. New York: Praeger.

Merideth, E. M., & Lotfipour, S. (1993). Reflecting through technology: A computer-laserdisc model of cooperative learning. *Journal of Technology and Teacher Education, 1*(1), 33-41.

Moore, M. G., Thompson, M. M., et al. (1990). The effects of distance learning: A summary of the literature. *The American Center for the Study of Distance Education, Research Monograph Number 2*. University Park: The Pennsylvania State University.

Posner, G. J. (1989). *Field experience: Methods of reflective teaching* (2nd ed). New York: Longman.

Reilly, B., Hull, G., & Greenleaf, C. (1993). Collaborative readings of hypermedia cases: A report on the development and testing of electronic portfolios to encourage inquiry in teacher education. *Journal of Technology and Teacher Education, 1*(1), 81-95.

Royce, P., Cummings, R., & Cheney, C. (1989). Project NETWORC: A distance learning model in early childhood special education. *Rural Special Education Quarterly, 10*(4), 2-4.

Sebastian, J. (1990). How do we keep them out in the field? Preparing special educators in rural school districts. *Journal of Navajo Education, 8*(2), 24-26.

Thompson, A., & Hayes, C. (1993). Patterns of use of an electronic communication network for student teachers and first year teachers. *Technology and Teacher Education Annual. Proceedings of the Fourth Annual Conference of the Society for Technology and Teacher Education* (pp. 680-683). Charlottesville, VA: The Association for the Advancement of Computing in Education.

Waugh, M. (1993). Illinois-U/C initiates electronic networking to enrich preservice and inservice teaching. *The Holmes Group Forum, 7*(3), 10-13.

❖ 7 ❖

Developing Leadership
in Preservice Teachers

SANDRA LEE GUPTON

School reform recommendations of the eighties were oftentimes focused on the reconceptualization of roles and responsibilities of school administrators and teachers. In an effort to abate the mediocrity of classrooms across the nation and to reform public education, teachers were targeted for greater participation in the decision making and leadership of their schools. The influential report of the Carnegie Task Force on Teaching as a Profession, *A Nation Prepared: Teachers for the 21st Century* (1986), included a recommendation for development of a corps of "lead teachers" in the profession who would assume leadership responsibilities in the schools. The report also called for teachers having "more control over their work environment" along with increased accountability. The terms *participatory style leadership* and *teacher empowerment* have become as commonplace as Chevrolet, apple pie, and the American flag, without adequate regard for how well teachers are prepared for or willing to participate in school-wide management and decision making. For teachers to assume greater responsibility for the decisions that have typically been the tasks of principals and administrators, there needs to be a reconceptualization of both teacher and administrator preparation programs to ensure inclusion of skills and content for educators to adapt to new roles and responsibilities. "Individuals and groups involved [in decision making] must be given sufficient training and adequate information to make decisions" (Gorton & Snowden, 1993, p. 24).

Programs of preparation for school administrators are currently under examination at state and national levels in an effort to redesign them for more rigor and compatibility with the reform recommendations for better-trained graduates with more team-based management skills; for example, the National Policy Board for Educational Administration's extensive document, *Principals for Our Changing Schools: Knowledge and Skill Base* (Thomson, 1993). "Although efforts are under way in many states to strengthen and tighten up requirements for the certification of school administrators," write Heller and Pautler in their work on the future of school leadership, "those who support the notion of empowerment feel that it is okay to turn over to teachers, many of whom have had no training in administration, the responsibility for managing our schools. Is this governance by those most naive about the system?" (1990, p. 141).

The Rationale for Shared Leadership in Education

Michael Fullan makes a strong case for reconceptualizing teacher professionalism by combining the teacher's historical "mantle of moral purpose with the skills of change agentry" (1993, p. 12). Fullan, Barth (1990), Teltel and O'Connor (1993), and other advocates of teacher empowerment contend that teachers will be unable to improve learning in their classrooms without helping to improve the surrounding school-wide context of the classroom— the historical "turfdom" of the chief-in-charge, the school principal.

The autocratic image of leadership holds little appeal or potential for achieving organizational excellence in today's world. Instead, the concept of shared leadership, in which all employees participate in making decisions about the running of the organization, has replaced the tightly controlled, hierarchical model of bureaucratic leadership espoused by Max Weber and practiced widely in this country during most of this century. "A strong leader who is in control, who must direct traffic at all crossroads of decisions, has no place in a school where all adults share responsibility in these areas" (Donaldson, 1993, p. 14).

The concept of shared leadership has been gaining momentum since the reform reports of the early eighties and proliferates within the current professional literature through an impressive and creative array of related terms such as *team leadership, collective decision making, interactive professionalism* (Fullan, 1993), *decentralization, distributed leadership* (Thurston, Clift, & Schacht, 1993), and *collaborative egalitarianism* (Duffy, 1994). Proponents of teacher empowerment and shared leadership claim that having teachers participate in school-based decision making will not only lead to better decisions but will also help to blur the "them" and "us" adversarial relationship that has traditionally existed between administrators and teachers; will replace the solitary authority of the principal with a more credible, collective authority; and will essentially facilitate the transformation of school environments into healthier, more pleasant places for children and adults (Barth, 1990). "The teacher of the future," writes Fullan, "must be equally at home in the classroom and in working with others to bring about continuous improvements" (1993, p. 17).

The whole notion of teachers having more ownership of programs, curricula, and school operations that they themselves must implement seems to be just good psychology. Whenever people feel that they are important to the organization and have input into making decisions about their own work, they are usually happier and more likely to work hard to make new ideas work. Maslow's hierarchy of needs and Herzberg's two-factor theory on job satisfaction are two well-accepted theories of human motivation supportive of the empowerment concept.

The concept of an empowered teaching force has led to a redefinition of teaching in which it emerges as a more professional, reflective occupation. *Reflective practitioner* and *constructivist* are two relatively new terms used to describe today's empowered teacher; these terms embody teacher behaviors characterized by professional autonomy and greater participation in organizational decision making. The constructivist teacher follows no prescriptions for successful teaching, acts as facilitator of meaning-making rather than leader of all learning, adapts to a variety of contexts affecting schooling, and is deeply involved in processes related to the purposes of education.

This new image of teaching is incompatible with autocratic, top-down administrative leadership. Petrie (1990) concludes, in his article on restructuring the teaching profession, that teachers must take over a considerable part of education's leadership:

> It seems clear that if teachers are to be viewed as reflective practitioners exercising professional judgment, educational leaders will not tell such professionals what to do. There will not be detailed syllabi externally imposed. Bureaucratic rules and regulations will be kept to a minimum. Structures will be developed that allow a broad range of discretion and influence . . . (pp. 21-22)

After all, central to the work of educators—teachers and administrators—is what is happening in the classroom. How can the best decisions be made for students without involving the people who work most closely with them? The case for shared leadership is easy to make; the difficulty comes in somehow making it work (see Figure 7.1).

Problems Encountered With
Shared Leadership in Education

Undeniably, the trendy popularity of empowered workers, decentralization, and site-based management in recent years has

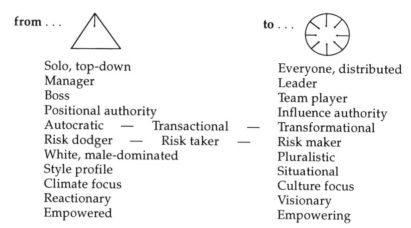

from . . .   to . . .

Solo, top-down   Everyone, distributed
Manager   Leader
Boss   Team player
Positional authority   Influence authority
Autocratic   —   Transactional   —   Transformational
Risk dodger   —   Risk taker   —   Risk maker
White, male-dominated   Pluralistic
Style profile   Situational
Climate focus   Culture focus
Reactionary   Visionary
Empowered   Empowering

Figure 7.1. Leadership's Paradigm Shifts

thus far resulted in more rhetoric than reality in the workplace. Much of the criticism from teachers regarding participatory decision making and shared leadership stems from their administrators' reluctance to involve them in meaningful leadership activities and substantive decisions. There is a growing recognition of the need to direct more attention to *what* decisions are being shared in addition to *who* is making the decision if the power of the administrator is truly to include teachers. Some decisions are clearly more important and relevant to teachers than are others. Decisions that relate to issues about which teachers care deeply are typically those that have an impact on the purposes, priorities, and practices of schools and education. For example, in their work with site-based management (SBM), Midgley and Wood (1993) contend that SBM can be effective in making substantive school reform only when it is viewed not as an end in itself, but as an "important process" that involves teachers in "making critical decisions that affect the very purposes and goals of education":

> Teachers have not traditionally been involved in [critical] decisions. . . . Compare the goal of developing a standardized format for student papers with the goal of replacing standardized tests with portfolios and other methods

> of work sampling. . . . It is easy to see how some schools
> could adopt the apparatus of SBM and declare their teach-
> ers to be "empowered" when there is no change of any
> consequence for students. (pp. 251-252)

But administrators are not wholly to blame for their reticence
to relinquish their authority in certain areas of the school's operation. As educators have attempted to adopt these newer participatory strategies, the highly bureaucratic, underlying structures of
the organization of schools have been stubbornly resistant to
changes in various organizational operations steeped in tradition
and cultural acceptance. In the eyes of many parents, students,
and teachers, the buck still stops at the principal's or superintendent's desk, though state law still places major legal responsibility
for the operation of schools on administrators' shoulders. Also,
many teachers themselves feel insecure about greater participation in school-wide decisions, because they have not the time, the
energy, nor the preparation for assuming such a role in the present
organization of schools. "It is no slander to say," comment Devaney
and Sykes (1988), "that many, many capable, long-experienced
teachers, upon pondering such obligations [increased professional-
level responsibilities] in return for professional salary and status,
might decline the offer—or would at least think twice before
accepting" (p. 3). The current push for systemic change evolved
from past school reform efforts that failed to encompass the basic
structures of the organization and were thereby short-circuited.
For radical reform in public education to occur, the system must
be changed, and the whole system covers a lot of territory. "If we
are to move to a new model of school reform," Darling-Hammond
(1993) asserts, "we must reframe the reform agenda by reducing
prescriptions for practice while investing in new forms of professional development, policy development, and political development" (p. 759). The soup-to-nuts approach to reforming the
system must be more fundamental and comprehensive than the
more typical, single-track emphases on changing parts and pieces
of the system without making simultaneous compatible adjust-
ments to the whole machine. Programs preparing teachers are a
vital part of the system and must be redesigned to facilitate the

emergent roles of teachers as true professionals, with powers of decision making about critical aspects of their work.

Innovative Programs of
Teacher Preparation for Leadership

In the midst of the school reform flurry in this nation, little change has occurred in the hallowed halls of higher education's teacher preparatory programs. In his definitive book, *A Place Called School*, Goodlad recommended in 1984 that programs of preparation for teachers be dramatically changed. He commented that, unfortunately, "little either in current practice or even in innovative stirrings" in teacher preparation could be found. "Teacher education programs are disturbingly alike and almost uniformly inadequate" (Goodlad, 1984, p. 315). Today, a full decade later, teacher education programs remain stubbornly resistant to internal reform efforts consistent with the K-12 reform movement. Current professional literature, however, reflects at least a growing awareness of the necessity for reform efforts to include higher education and its programs of preparation for teachers and administrators. For example, Darling-Hammond (1993) calls attention to the urgent need to develop new forms of preservice and ongoing professional development to support "the type of practitioner knowledge that can inform teachers' judgments in complex situations. . . . School reform efforts must focus on building the capacity of schools and teachers to undertake tasks they have never before been called upon to accomplish" (pp. 754-759). "Faculties of education," writes Fullan (1993), "must redesign their programs to focus directly on developing the beginner's knowledge base for effective teaching *and* the knowledge base for changing the conditions that affect teaching" (p. 16). Robinson and Sandhop (1993) make a case for revamping programs of preparation for administrators in order to accommodate major reform efforts that call for new leadership roles for administrators and teachers. "The implication for practitioners," they write, "is that preparation must reflect increasing levels of understanding and sensitivity to these changing organizational relationships . . .

from . . .	to . . .
Technician	Professional
Prescribed	Constructed
Defensive	Responsible
Direction-taker	Decision-maker
Solo player	Collaborator
Lesson planner	School improvement planner
Reactive	Reflective
Implementor	Initiator
Research consumer	Action researcher
Follower	Empowered

Figure 7.2. Teaching's Paradigm Shifts

and their ramifications for providing leadership" (p. 7). Though Robinson and Sandhop particularly address the need to restructure programs of higher education for prospective administrators, certainly no less should be undertaken for the other players in the arena of shared leadership—the teachers. Teachers as well as administrators must be trained and educated for a form of organizational participation very different from the models that most higher education curricula use to prepare them (see Figure 7.2).

Although innovative programs of teacher preparation are few, some attempts are being made to redesign programs to be more compatible with the emerging role of teachers as greater participants in school- and system-level decision making and as key players in school reform efforts. The Puget Sound Educational Consortium is an example of a school/university partnership between the University of Washington and 12 Seattle-area school districts. This group initially worked on investigating dimensions of teacher leadership, which eventually led to the collaborative construction of new roles for teachers (Lieberman & McLaughlin, 1992). Although this project focused on practicing teachers, there are profound implications for its potential to have an impact on preservice teachers as well. Improved communication and collaboration between schools and universities have the capacity to help practicing educators while simultaneously giving impetus and input to university faculty for redesigning and updating their programs of preparation to enable teachers and administrators to assume changing roles in the organization of today's schools.

Another innovative program is the University of Wyoming's experimentation with greater collaboration between its undergraduate teacher education and educational leadership programs. Undergraduate students are screened and selected for participation in the "teacher leader" program, a program designed by both departments to foster leadership potential among promising preservice teachers and to facilitate a 10-week, full-time administrative internship in the principalship for graduate students in educational leadership. Undergraduate students selected for the program provide release time for the graduate students and, as a part of their training, participate in a teacher leadership class taught by faculty in the department of educational leadership.

Such interaction between undergraduate teacher preparation programs and educational administration departments is sorely needed to consistently and cooperatively redesign program curricula to reflect changing roles for all educators, to give prospective teachers and administrators opportunities to begin to learn to work together, to share the multiple resources of both departments, and to have the university graduate and undergraduate faculties practicing and being role models for the kind of coordination and collaboration espoused for and essential to shared leadership among the professional educators in K-12 schools.

At the University of Southern Maine, graduate students in the School for Professional Education are in the schools and classrooms every day, and even take university classes in local school buildings. Students interact constantly with both university faculty and practicing classroom teachers, which, according to Cherie Major, a professor in the program, has mutually benefited the schools and the university. "As a result of working with the schools, our college has done a lot of internal changes—in terms of what we value" (U.S. Department of Education, 1994).

Student teachers at The University of Southern Mississippi spend at least a part of their internship shadowing an administrator in the system. According to the director of field experiences at USM, Gloria A. Slick (October, 1994), the primary reason for including this as a part of student teachers' internship is to help them understand the total school operation, as well as the numbers and kinds of decisions that must be made in the organization of schools. Prospective teachers need a wide range of exposure to and involvement in the complex nature of leadership and school-wide decision making if they are to be best prepared to assume participation in these processes—even at a rudimentary level as a beginning teacher.

In their work with case studies of clinical supervision, Nolan, Hawkes, and Francis (1993) describe a process for clinical supervision of student teachers that has, as its number one goal, the autonomy of the teacher. "The goal," they state, "is for the teacher to become more self-directed and analytical. Collegiality, long-term observation, and reflection are the hallmarks of successful clinical supervision" (p. 53). With this form of student-teacher supervision, the student is the ultimate decision maker about his own teaching; the supervisor merely facilitates the analysis of those decisions. Helping student teachers to assume early in their practice the responsibility for constructing their own knowledge is consistent with the kinds of skills needed for classroom teachers to become true change agents and reflective professionals capable of sharing in school-wide leadership.

Conclusions and Recommendations

Roland Barth defines leadership as "making happen what you believe in" (1988, p. 131). The innovative programs of teacher preparation described above exemplify this kind of leadership: having the courage and commitment to initiate change and to tackle difficult problems for the betterment of the profession, including the adults as well as the students. Furthermore, these programs illustrate the variation in approaches and the many dimensions to which universities should give deliberate attention in an effort to provide more relevant, appropriate preparation for teachers as leaders.

Revamping total programs of teacher preparation involves three dimensions for consideration: (1) the *curriculum* (both content and pedagogy); (2) *collaboration and articulation* (between graduate and undergraduate departments of education; among universities, local schools and districts, and state departments of education; and between colleges of education and other colleges involved in preparing teachers); and (3) the *field-based and internship experiences* of preservice teachers. All three dimensions are interrelated and must be included in systemic reform of programs of teacher preparation. For the purposes of this book, however, the following recommendations are focused on the last dimension, the student teaching or preservice field experiences of education programs, in order to develop more strategically the leadership potential required of true professionals sharing organizational decision making:

Early identification and special placement of outstanding leadership potential. Faculties of educational administration and teacher preparation should work together to nurture leadership of all prospective teachers and administrators. Exceptional leadership talent could be identified early and nurtured with special counseling, program planning, and specifically designed field experiences.

Increased interaction between interning administrators and teachers. Throughout the entire programs of preparation as well as during internships, prospective administrators and teachers should have opportunities to begin to learn to work together and to share cooperatively problem-solving activities.

Increased use of student cohort groups. Participatory decision making requires many skills that are best learned by working as a member of a group. Students assigned to cohort groups for classes may also benefit from continuing the group experience as a part of the internship experience: being assigned to the same school or frequently sharing their experiences in seminars, by networking, or through regularly scheduled meetings.

Increased use of professional development schools. Careful placement of students for field experiences has long been recognized as critical to the success of internships.

To nurture leadership skills and attitudes among prospective teachers, it becomes even more important that students be given an environment wherein they have good role models and where they feel a part of the total school operation, with encouragement to contribute their ideas, the freedom to make mistakes, and the opportunity to take risks in an effort to grow and become more capable, reflective professionals.

More emphasis on action research. Leadership skills for educators cannot be optimally developed without teachers learning more about the procedures and value of classroom-based, practitioner-initiated research. True reflective practice demands action research; incorporating more research activities and projects into the internship experiences of preservice teachers would help them develop the skills and attitudes needed to continue this practice as teachers. Such reflective, professional practice is indicative of what is needed for outstanding leadership in continued school-improvement initiatives.

Providing more frequent and more differentiated, developmentally appropriate field-based experiences. Throughout teacher preparation programs, students should have opportunities to be in the schools for a variety of reasons that will help make their academic work more relevant and meaningful. Because of the wide variation in backgrounds and abilities of most student populations and their individual career goals, it makes sense that their needs for field-based experiences would also vary widely.

Better differentiation among students and more frequent experiences in the schools and classrooms would enhance opportunities for prospective teachers to tap their potential for success in all areas of the profession, including their individual leadership potential.

Increased emphasis on peer- and self-evaluation. For teachers to be capable of sharing in organizational decisions, they should surely be able to critique themselves and share in the assessment of their peers' teaching performance. Increased emphasis on student teachers' self-assessment and evaluation of their peers should enhance their confidence and increase their ability to make decisions that will contribute to school-wide operations for the ultimate benefit of students. Supervision that falls in the "coaching" category seems more appropriate for preparing the leaders of tomorrow's schools than the more traditional models, which focus on evaluation over growth and development of skills and methods.

Increased reliance on constructivist strategies during the internship. Techniques that help student teachers to become more analytical and reflective practitioners should also make them better participants in school-wide decision making. Engaging students in reflective dialogues about their teaching, having them keep journals of their reactions to their experiences, including more micro-teaching experiences during their internships, and helping them become better self-critics and less dependent on outside feedback will contribute significantly to their potential for passing these skills along to their students, and to their ability and confidence to share in the leadership responsibilities of their schools. Such internship experiences for preservice teachers should ultimately lead to schools becoming better, more reflective places for everyone.

To redesign interrelated dimensions of teacher preparation to facilitate the development of a new breed of teachers who are autonomous, reflective professionals capable of participating in school-wide leadership, however, the very culture of schools of education in higher education must change to reflect the new professionalism espoused for teaching. An essential first step in this change process is improving the quality of the university faculty. Better-qualified faculty, with a strong track record of public school experience, are needed in schools of education, both to be effective in their roles as teachers and supervisors of teachers and to have the credibility and understanding needed to work successfully with public school personnel. Additionally, university administration and faculty must approach the work of reforming teacher education with new perspectives, higher expectations, and greater respect for their roles and the whole education profession, and with a sense of urgency and importance rarely demonstrated in revision efforts in higher education. For the dynamic changes needed in revamping programs of teacher preparation to meet the profession's new challenges of leadership and reflective practice, the faculty in colleges of education must be exceptional themselves and exemplary of the new professional educators they are responsible for nurturing.

References

Barth, R. S. (1988). School: A community of leaders. In A. Lieberman (Ed.), *Building a professional culture in schools* (pp. 129-147). New York: Teachers College Press.

Barth, R. S. (1990). *Improving schools from within*. San Francisco: Jossey-Bass.

Basom, P. (1993, Fall). Educational leadership faculty involved in teacher education: Unholy alliance or advancement of the mission? *Connections: Conversations on Issues of Principal Preparation, 2*(1), 3.

Carnegie Task Force on Teaching as a Profession. (1986). *A nation prepared: Teachers for the 21st century*. New York: Author.

Darling-Hammond, L. (1993). Reframing the school reform agenda. *Phi Delta Kappan, 74*(10), 753-759.

Devaney, K., & Sykes, G. (1988). Making the case for professionalism. In A. Lieberman (Ed.), *Building a professional culture in schools* (pp. 3-21). New York: Teachers College Press.

Donaldson, G. A. (1993). Working smarter together. *Educational Leadership, 51*(2), 12-16.

Duffy, G. G. (1994). Professional development schools and the disempowerment of teachers and professors. *Phi Delta Kappan, 75*(8), 596-601.

Fullan, M. G. (1993). Why teachers must become change agents. *Educational Leadership, 50*(6), 12-17.

Goodlad, J. I. (1984). *A place called school: Prospects for the future*. New York: McGraw-Hill.

Gorton, R., & Snowden, P. E. (1993). *School leadership and administration* (4th ed.). Madison, WI: Brown & Benchmark.

Heller, R. W., & Pautler, A. J. (1990). The administrator of the future: Combining instructional and managerial leadership. In S. L. Jacobson & J. A. Conway (Eds.), *Educational leadership in an age of reform* (p. 131-143). New York: Longman.

Lieberman, A., & McLaughlin, M. W. (1992). Networks for educational change: Powerful and problematic. *Phi Delta Kappan, 73*(9), 673-677.

Midgley, C., & Wood, S. (1993). Beyond site-based management: Empowering teachers to reform schools. *Phi Delta Kappan, 75*(3), 245-252.

Nolan, J., Hawkes, B., & Francis, P. (1993). Case studies: Windows onto clinical supervision. *Educational Leadership, 51*(2), 52-56.

Petrie, H. G. (1990). Reflections on the second wave of reform: Restructuring the teaching profession. In S. L. Jacobson & J. A. Conway (Eds.), *Educational leadership in an age of reform* (pp. 14-29). New York: Longman.

Robinson, L. A., & Sandhop, B. J. (1993, Fall). Cooperative integrated administration for organizational structuring. *Connections: Conversations on Issues of Principal Preparation, 2*(1), 7-9.

Teltel, L., & O'Connor, K. (1993, Fall). Teachers as leaders: Implications for the preparation of principals. *Connections: Conversations on Issues of Principal Preparation, 2*(1), 1, 6, 7.

Thomson, S. D. (Ed.). (1993). *Principals for our changing schools: Knowledge and skill base.* Fairfax, VA: National Policy Board for Educational Administration.

Thurston, P., Clift, R., & Schacht, M. (1993). Preparing leaders for change-oriented schools. *Phi Delta Kappan, 75*(3), 259-265.

U.S. Department of Education. (1994). *America 2000: Community update.* Washington, DC: Author.

❖ 8 ❖

What Happens
After Student Teaching

The First Five Years

GENEVIEVE BROWN
BEVERLY J. IRBY

With student teaching behind you, the excitement wells as you think of your first "real" teaching experience, with your own students on your own class roster and in your own classroom; but, as Dickens wrote, "it was the best of times, it was the worst of times." And so it is. On one hand, you are filled with excitement; on the other, you are probably a little nervous about being responsible for facilitating a whole year's worth of learning for young people. This chapter, designed as a thought-provoking guide, will assist you in your new adventure of teaching by discussing beginning teacher needs, mentoring relationships, student-teacher relationships, peer relationships, pitfalls to avoid, and your professional growth from the first through the fifth years.

The Unique Nature of the Teaching Profession

There are several points unique to the nature of our profession. First, you will find that much of your workday is spent in isolation from your peers. This is much different from other professions, where supervisors and coworkers are beside the new employee, giving ongoing guidance. Second, you may find yourself with difficult teaching assignments. Often beginning teachers have multiple preparations, challenging students, students with diverse backgrounds, lack of parental support, many extracurricular assignments, and committee work. Because of these unique features of our profession and because many times we must teach in adverse conditions, you should never feel bashful about asking for assistance. Many times experienced teachers will not initiate offering suggestions because they may feel that they are intruding or interfering. During your student teaching, you had support from several sources who were there to nurture you and build your self-confidence. As you move from student to teacher, you may feel that you are on your own and alone. But you are not alone; lesson number one for the beginning teacher: Ask questions and seek assistance.

Finding Assistance

Many schools have induction programs for beginning teachers. An induction program is a program in which beginning teachers have a year-long introduction to the teaching profession, through the assistance of mentor teachers and the participation of special staff development. If the school has an induction program, you will be assigned a mentor teacher.

As soon as you sign your contract, ask your principal, team leader, or department chair if your school participates in a mentor program. If not, ask your supervisor if you can be assigned a mentor teacher to advise and assist you during your transition year.

Your Mentor Teacher

What is a mentor teacher? How can a mentor teacher help? Your supervising teacher during your student teaching experience was a type of mentor. The general function of a mentor is to assist an apprentice in moving from beginner-level knowledge to that of a more advanced and accomplished practitioner. Specifically, a mentor teacher is a master teacher who is willing to be helpful and share effective teaching practices, time-management skills, curriculum organization, and discipline-management techniques with a novice teacher. He or she may also assist you in locating materials, setting up your classroom, getting started on the first few days of school, reviewing your lessons for effectiveness, and grouping of students for instruction. Your mentor will also help you in learning the culture of your school. He or she will assist you in knowing how to dress, where to go for duty or for lunch, or a simple thing like where to get pencils or notepads. As you get more established, your mentor can help you by coming into your classroom and offering tips for more effective teaching. Take this as constructive criticism and carefully consider how you will use the suggestions for improving your instruction to enhance student learning.

You and Your Mentor—The Mentoring Relationship

Your mentor will be a very special person of whom you will grow very fond over the years. At first you may have a little anxiety about working with your mentor. You may wonder what your mentor expects of you and what standards he or she has for you. The best way to find out is to sit down and talk through expectations. You may have some expectations you wish to share as well. You may have fears that the mentor will not allow you to be creative or to use your own initiative. The mentor is there to facilitate your growth, not to turn you into a clone of him or her. Keep that in mind as you work with your mentor.

Because you will be working so closely with your mentor, you may wish to get to know him or her a little better. Find out his or her special interests, characteristics, and likes and dislikes. Find out when his or her birthday is and do something special.

You may be concerned about making mistakes. Don't worry, you will. All people make mistakes. Your mentor will be there for you and will not criticize you for making a mistake. Rather, your mentor will help you celebrate those mistakes. Yes, celebrate mistakes—for through our mistakes, we grow.

Information You Need to Know

Remember that your mentor is there to help you and is a valuable resource. Take advantage of that wealth of knowledge and experience. Following are a few general questions new teachers frequently ask their mentors. You will undoubtedly generate many questions relevant to your particular campus setting during the first few days and weeks. Jot down your questions and don't be hesitant to ask them.

How should my classroom and schedule be organized for the beginning of school?

How can I develop a set of rules and procedures for my classroom that will be consistent with campus policy?

How can I make my students accountable?

What kind of activities would be appropriate for the first week of school?

What is the management system that has served you best?

What is a good way to organize instruction?

How do you handle grading, taking roll, and paperwork?

What do you suggest for bulletin boards at the beginning of school?

When would be a good time for me to visit in your classroom?

Are there other teachers who would be good role models for me to visit?

Where are the curriculum guides? Do we use curriculum guides?

What are district policies and procedures I need to know?

What should I know about local teacher organizations, insurance, and extra pay for extra duties or staff development?

Do we give annual standardized tests? Where are the objectives? How do I align the objectives with my classroom curriculum or lessons?

How do I get parents involved?

When can we meet again? Will our meetings be regularly scheduled in the future?

When should you ask these questions? We suggest that you schedule a meeting with your mentor before school starts. He or she will be busy getting school started as well, so be sure to regard his or her time as valuable. You do not have to be afraid of using your mentor's time; simply be sure that when you have serious questions for beginning school, time is allocated and scheduled. Getting your questions answered before school starts will help you operate at an advantage. You will feel more confident in knowing school procedures, and you can have things arranged in your room so that you'll have more time to get familiar with the faculty members with whom you will work. You will definitely want to introduce yourself to the secretarial staff, the custodians, the counselor, the librarians, the support staff, and the nurse.

Because you will want to know as much as possible about your campus, spend some time reading the school handbook. What is the total enrollment? Who are the instructional aides and how can they help you and your students? Is there a parent organization? What are your hours? What are the staff development or in-service dates? How much are you allotted for supplies? Is the campus supply room open, or is it open only to the secretary? What are the hours you can work after regular school hours? What are other responsibilities that faculty have? Are there any regularly used forms? What are the lunchroom procedures? Do you have field trips, and what are the policies? These are all questions that can be answered by office personnel, through your school handbook, by your mentor, or by other experienced teachers.

Your Professional and Personal Needs

It is natural for a new teacher to feel concern over several issues, at both a professional level and a personal level. So that you know you are not alone, we have included below some needs beginning teachers have expressed (Veenman, 1984). They are concerned about student learning, getting students to learn, and student satisfaction. Managing the classroom, relating to students' parents and the school community, feeling isolated, refining their existing teaching skills, and learning rules and procedures for the campus and district are also major concerns. On a personal level, the beginning teachers indicated a need to separate from the past and to develop their own identity as an adult and as a teacher, to build new social relationships, to learn new roles, to balance their work and home life, and to be valued by their friends and the community for the work they do. These concerns and feelings are normal; you are not alone if you have them. Be sure that you are not alone in dealing with these feelings; you will have your mentor and other beginning teachers with whom you can confer.

Dealing With Stress

One other problem you may face during the first year, and particularly during the first months of school, is stress. One study (Earl, 1993) reported that the greatest stressors of first-year elementary teachers were (1) administrators and communication, (2) discipline, (3) teacher evaluation, and (4) instruction/curriculum.

In dealing with stress in any profession or situation, it is recommended that the first step in coping with stress is to identify the source of stress (Earl, 1993). Other helpful tips for coping with stress include making sure you allow time for recreational activities, maintaining healthy eating and sleeping habits, and establishing and maintaining a regular physical exercise routine. If you find that you are experiencing extreme stress, discuss this with your mentor, or perhaps with your school counselor. They will have additional suggestions.

Working With Students

During your student teaching experience and in your course work, you will extensively discuss motivation, establishing a positive climate, and addressing the needs of diverse classroom populations. Following is a brief discussion of more salient points to remember in working with students effectively. Positive classroom climate is an important factor to consider when motivating students to learn. When students are in a classroom that is pleasant and invites participation through active involvement, they are much more likely to be cooperative and to attend to learning tasks. Students who are on task are not as likely to cause behavioral problems; thus, a positive classroom climate is a key to preventive discipline, which facilitates learning.

Certainly, an important aspect of climate is the physical appearance of your room. Students respond positively to a neat and attractive environment. You will want to have colorful bulletin boards, posters, and displays in your room from the very first day. Many successful teachers strive to create a homelike atmosphere in their classroom, where they place rugs, rocking chairs, large pillows, sofas, lamps, and attractive artwork. Seasonal displays are always welcomed by students as are displays of their work. In addition, many successful teachers make sure that all materials and supplies are kept available for students including extra pens, pencils, markers, paper, tissues, and the like, in the event students fail to bring these to class. This not only invites students to learn, it also gives them a secure feeling. In addition, it is an effective time-saving measure, because it eliminates their having to go through desks or lockers in search of materials. This also prevents confrontations with the students.

Another important aspect of inviting students to succeed and creating a positive school climate is giving them clear and realistic expectations. It is important for students to know the rules and procedures from the first day of class. Many effective teachers post classroom rules and consequences in prominent locations in the classroom and allow students to assist in the development of those rules and consequences. It is also important that teachers learn students' names very quickly.

Teachers who develop a positive classroom climate tend to encourage student interaction and student questions; practice friendly and courteous behavior such as smiling, reinforcing efforts frequently, and showing care and concern for students' personal lives; and let students know that there are no dumb questions and that it is all right to make mistakes.

A positive classroom will respect individuals. Effective teachers are able to appreciate and celebrate diversity in cultures, languages, genders, learning styles, and levels of achievement. They model respectful behaviors and expect the students to do the same.

Working With Colleagues, Administrators, and Parents

It is important that during the first few years of teaching you become known as a professional, dedicated educator. You will want to project a positive attitude and a professional image. Your mentor will be of great assistance to you in this area of your career. The following brief comments will be helpful for your first year, as well as in subsequent years.

Colleagues

Many beginning teachers have remarked about the importance of positive role models. Though your mentor should be a good role model for you, there will be other outstanding and highly respected teachers on the campus who will also be positive examples. Notice what these successful and credible teachers do, not only in terms of their classrooms, but also how they relate to other teachers, parents, and students and how they project a professional image. To further ensure that your colleagues accept you into the culture of the campus and view you as a professional, you should remember several points:

1. Be on time for your duty (you will be liable for injuries during your duty time).
2. Arrive at school early and stay late (30 to 45 minutes).
3. Do your part on committees and special projects.
4. Be a good observer and a good listener (don't talk too much about victories or defeats).
5. Meet all deadlines.
6. Be consistent and fair with students.
7. Be yourself.
8. Seek and accept suggestions and advice from others.
9. Request teachers' permission to use their ideas and recognize them for their ideas.
10. Be sure to do what you are expected to do. (Page, 1991)

Administrators

Your school principal and assistant principal are key people on your campus, and the principal will be your primary evaluator. These administrators will be very busy, but they will be interested in seeing you succeed; therefore, they, as well as your mentor, will be available to assist you. Just as you respect the time of your mentor, you should also respect the busy schedule of your administrators. The following tips will help enhance your reputation as a professional and gain the respect of administrators:

1. Turn in administrative requests on time (reports, report cards, lesson plans).
2. Be sure to apprise your administrator of any problems you may be having with students or parents.
3. Follow all procedures on your campus. In the event that there are procedures you may not agree with, do not complain about them. Rather, when the appropriate time arises, you may wish to ask your mentor the reason for the guidelines or discuss your concerns in a professional manner. Or perhaps, you may wish to be a problem solver and work on a task force to change the procedures if the occasion arises.

Always remember that it is better to be a problem solver than a problem starter.

4. Your administrators can assist you in improving your instruction; take the criticism positively, and don't become defensive and never place blame on others for your mistakes. Know that failures can result in growth. Always try to analyze why a mistake or a failure occurred, and determine what you can do to change the situation or improve the next time.

5. During faculty meetings and staff development sessions, be courteous and give your full attention to the speaker or facilitator. It is unprofessional and rude to read or grade papers during this time.

6. Be respectful to your administrators. Don't burden them with your personal problems unless they particularly inquire. Personal problems are better handled in the counselor's office or with your mentor (Page, 1991).

Parents

Parents can be your strongest allies. You will want to enlist their support early to ensure that you are all on the team that is pulling for the child. Schedule parent conferences early. Before the parents arrive, you will want to develop a plan for the conference—much like you develop your lesson plans. Have a specific agenda with specific questions you wish to ask the parents. If you are having a problem, have a tentative plan to share, but also enlist the assistance of the parents in the solution.

During the conference let the tone of your voice and your action during the conference let the parent know you care. Never judge the child, label the child, or compare the child to others.

Because you will have a limited time for the conference, you want to keep the conference moving by staying on task and sticking to your agenda. Make sure that parents understand what you are saying and that you understand them and the concerns they have about their child. You may use a feedback technique during the conference such as, "Now, this is what I hear you saying . . . is that correct?" End the conference positively, giving parents hope regarding their child. If there are problems or tensions during the conference, you might want to stop the conference and reschedule within 3 days. This may give some time for tempers to cool and additional information to be gathered (Page, 1991). It is a good idea to keep a parent conference folder on each child so that phone conferences and school conferences can be kept on record. Any plans should also be documented in the record. At least three conferences throughout the year are suggested for each child.

Encourage ongoing communication with parents, because parents can be a great help to you in a number of ways: as partners in their child's development, as problem solvers, as a real audience for presentations, as supporters and volunteers in the classroom, as advisors on classroom and school policy, and as community supporters (Petrzelka, 1992).

Pitfalls and Perils of the First 5 Years

According to beginning teachers, the first 5 years can be perilous if teachers are not aware of the importance of time management, role models, and professionalism. Effective time management will help you avoid a major pitfall. Although there are many training programs and materials on effective time management, the following few simple guidelines are a good start:

1. Plan and organize your lessons; make sure that all materials have been ordered and are in stock before you start a new unit.
2. Close your door when you are involved in curriculum/ lesson development, grading, or other types of paperwork.
3. When you are on a deadline, let your colleagues know in a nice, but firm manner.
4. Respond to memos at the bottom of the original communication.
5. Document your return calls to parents or others—try once, then send a note home—after that, the other party is obligated to return the call or the note to you.

Another pitfall to avoid is negative role models. Associate with positive people. They will make your day more pleasant and will fill you with more enthusiasm. Try to remain positive.

One related pitfall is negative lounge talk. You will want to be sociable with your colleagues; however, if negative or unprofessional conversations are taking place in the lounge, then the best thing to do is stay away.

Being around individuals who are negative can sometimes lead you to be negative and even initiate negative self-talk. You will want to be aware of this. Listen to your inner thoughts. What are you saying to yourself? Are you saying, "I can't get these students to learn or behave"? Or are you saying, "I know I can do this"? You will need to speak positively to yourself. Keep telling yourself—"I can!"

Unfortunately, you may encounter teachers who have a lax professional image. Avoid the pitfall of allowing them to influence you. Display a positive and professional image at all times. Your manner of dress can assist in communicating this professional image (Irby-Davis & Brown, 1992). You will remember from your student teaching the importance of dressing as a professional rather than as a student. You will also remember the importance of not losing your temper, cursing, or using sarcasm.

Ethical behavior is a must for teachers. Many professional organizations and states publish codes of ethics for educators. Ask your mentor or principal for a copy.

Even experienced or veteran teachers make mistakes. During your first few years of teaching, you may feel that you are making so many mistakes that you will never get it right (oops—negative self-talk). Do not get discouraged. Celebrate your mistakes as opportunities for growth.

Assessing Effectiveness

Successful and productive teachers engage frequently in self-assessment and reflection; true professionals are learners who set specific goals for continuing to learn and grow. They consistently analyze their lessons, and their interactions with students, colleagues, and others, in an objective manner, and determine steps for improvement. You will want to get into the habit of taking a few moments at the end of each day to review events and activities that went well, along with those that were not so positive or successful. Be very honest with yourself. Recognize that even the best of teachers can "blow a lesson" or make a mistake in dealing with a situation. Decide specifically what you will do differently tomorrow or if a similar situation occurs again. If it is appropriate, make amends or take corrective action immediately and then move on. Determine to be solution-oriented rather than problem-oriented.

Be sure to keep notes, a log, a journal, or daily reflections so that you can use this for an action plan or to set long-term goals, if appropriate. Perhaps you have your students keep portfolios, or you may have developed a portfolio as a student. Many teachers build professional portfolios, which include examples of their work and activities with reflections. Keeping your own professional portfolio will document your growth and indicate areas of needed improvement.

Professional Growth

Documenting your professional growth, as discussed above, can assist you in becoming a more effective teacher, in self-assessment, or in gaining a new position. One way to assess your professional growth is through videotaping teaching segments throughout the year and analyzing your own instructional patterns.

Other ways to grow professionally include joining professional organizations, reading their journals, and attending their meetings. Take advantage of opportunities to attend workshops to gain new and effective practices. Additionally, networking and peer coaching with teachers who are on the same grade level or in the same field can be beneficial, because you share common concerns and problem solve together.

Your Future

As you consider future plans within the profession, you will recognize that a commitment to professional growth is essential. Marking a career path is an important aspect of this commitment. The development of a career path frequently involves talking to and observing teachers, supervisors, and administrators whom you admire. Asking them about their journeys through the profession can assist you in planning your path. Because most individuals in education who are successful have advanced degrees or additional certification or endorsements, you will want to consider pursuing an advanced degree. Some universities offer course work at the school district site; take advantage of this opportunity.

Becoming a Leader

When you are seen as knowledgeable, creative, persistent, hardworking, and committed, then you are on your way to becoming a leader in the profession. Setting some goals toward being an effective teacher is an important step toward becoming a leader. Your first year is critical and your next 4 years will move you closer to becoming the leading teacher who has the potential to make a difference in our educational system.

References

Earl, J. C. (May, 1993). *The relationship between career development and stress in elementary teachers.* Unpublished doctoral dissertation, Texas A&M University.

Irby-Davis, B., & Brown, G. (1992, June). Your interview image. *The Executive Educator, 14*(6).

Page, R. (1991). *Mentors: Who are they and what do they do?* Midland, TX: Region XVIII Education Service Center.

Petrzelka, V. (1992). *Tomball independent school district teacher induction program.* Tomball, TX: Tomball Independent School District.

Veenman, S. (1984). Perceived problems of beginning teachers. *Review of Educational Research, 54*(2), 143-178.

❖ 9 ❖

Learning From
International Field Experiences

LAURA L. STACHOWSKI
JAMES M. MAHAN

Reviews of the literature on student teaching (Guyton & McIntyre, 1990; Hersh, Hull, & Leighton, 1982; Lanier & Little, 1986) reveal that a predictable set of desired learnings is the focus of most student teaching assignments. Cooperating classroom teachers and university supervisors typically join forces to ensure that the student teachers in their charge acquire the skills, techniques, and attitudes that enable them to function competently in the instructional, managerial, and disciplinary capacities defining a teacher's role. Although such student teacher learnings are undeniably significant and should continue to receive considerable attention during the student teaching experience, emphasizing them alone tends to foster an undesirably narrow view in prospective educators of what teaching—*and learning*—are all about. Student teach-

99

ers must be encouraged, indeed required, to venture beyond the walls of their assigned classrooms, beyond the grounds of their elementary or secondary schools, and into the community and world of which schools are a part, and which schools should partially shape.

Increasingly, schools of education are recognizing the need for programs that will inculcate teacher trainees with the means to promote cross-cultural and international literacy in their class-rooms; yet, according to Pickert (1992), education majors are among the least likely students in higher education to enroll in courses with cross-cultural or international emphases. "The chal-lenge," wrote Pickert, "is to deliver graduates who are competent not only to function professionally in an international environ-ment, but who are equipped to make personal and public-policy decisions as citizens of an international society" (1992, p. iii). This notion reinforces Benjamin's (1985) earlier assertion: "The fact that we are each global citizens first must be the central philosophical point from which all teachers operate" (p. 81). However, Zimpher (1989) reported that most preservice educators possess a "limited cultural world view" and "modest diversity of cultural experi-ence," thus amplifying the complexities surrounding Pickert's challenge.

Perhaps the most effective programs geared toward promot-ing cross-cultural and international literacy are those that actually immerse prospective educators into other cultures in other nations for teaching and community involvement internships. Bennett (1990) identified "cultural immersion" as the mode for achieving the highest level of cross-cultural awareness: "awareness of how another culture feels from the standpoint of the insider" (p. 292). However, Wilson (1982) warned that merely being in a culturally different setting does not necessarily result in a cross-cultural or international perspective. She believed that "persons are more likely to learn from experience when they are prepared for the experience, engage in educational activities during that experi-ence, and evaluate the experience" (p. 185).

The purposes of this chapter are to describe a successful inter-national field experience program based on preparation, on-site academic assignments, and follow-up and evaluation, and to identify several important learnings and insights that have been gained by the preservice participants as a result of their cultural immersion experiences.

The Overseas Student Teaching Project

The Overseas Student Teaching Project has been implemented for the past 19 years by Indiana University. Offered as an optional supplement to conventional student teaching, this popular project has prepared and placed more than 750 student teachers for teaching assignments in the schools of England, Scotland, Wales, the Republic of Ireland, Australia, and New Zealand. Persons receiving certification in elementary and secondary education have participated, as well as those receiving "all grades" certification in music, special education, art, and physical education. During the academic year prior to student teaching, project participants are required to undergo extensive preparation (including seminars, readings, abstracts, papers, and workshops) on the educational practices and cultural values, beliefs, and lifestyles operating in the placement sites for which they have applied. These requirements not only familiarize the student teachers with the schools and cultures of which they will become a part but also serve as effective self-screening and staff selection steps, in that applicants who may want only to play tourist are discouraged by the intensive preparatory work.

During the student teaching semester, project participants must first teach in-state for a minimum of 10 weeks to receive certification; they then spend at least 8 weeks in their host nations, where they live with families in the communities and teach in national primary and secondary schools. Overseas school sites are arranged by the Foundation for International Education, which provides this placement service for numerous institutions in the United States (Korsgaard, 1994). While at their sites, project participants are expected to engage fully in all teacher-related functions of the school, form friendships with community people and become involved in their activities, interview people from diverse walks of life, and submit reflective reports identifying local attitudes, cultural values, world issues, and personal and professional insights (for a more thorough account of the Overseas Project, see Mahan & Stachowski, 1985).

Important Learnings and Insights Reported by Student Teachers as a Result of International Field Assignments

What are some of the learnings acquired by student teachers abroad? How do international field experiences benefit novice educators in ways that conventional student teaching assignments typically do not?

Number and Content of Learnings. Near the conclusion of their student teaching experiences, 63 Overseas Project participants and 28 "conventional," in-state student teachers were asked to reflect upon, identify, and record *new learnings* they judged to be of extreme personal and/or professional importance. These learnings were grouped under the following categories: Classroom Teaching Strategies, Curriculum Content and Selection, Fact Acquisition, Human Interrelationships, Discoveries About Self, World Human Life/Global Issues, Aesthetic Knowledge/Appreciation, and Miscellaneous. A total of 1,688 learnings were identified by the project participants, averaging about 27 per respondent, as compared to 548 learnings for the conventional student teachers, with an average of about 20 each.

A number of noteworthy trends emerged from these data. First, student teachers who had participated in international field experiences reported a greater number of important learnings overall than did their conventional student teacher counterparts. Every category had a higher frequency of learnings acquired by those individuals who had completed teaching, living, and community involvement experiences in culturally different environments. Second, only 29.2% of these learnings were classified by overseas respondents into the Classroom Teaching Strategies and Curriculum Content/Selection categories, which are the common foci for teacher education courses. Conventional student teachers, on the other hand, classified 37.1% of their learnings under these categories. Vital as such skills and knowledge are to effective teaching, they need not rule out other important learnings of a different nature that can be garnered by participants during the student teaching experience. A third trend is that overseas respondents emphasized the remaining categories more heavily than did the conventional student teachers, whose greater concerns were with curriculum and teaching methodology. The more extensive and diverse factual and affective learnings acquired by overseas participants are typically not addressed in conventional student teaching, nor are novice educators generally required to engage in activities that would make such learnings possible. Yet, the student teachers for whom these learnings became a reality attached major personal importance to them. Discoveries about the self and the relationship of the self with others and with the world appear to be highly valued, suggesting that significant learning does occur outside the classroom when it is structured into an existing student teaching program (Mahan & Stachowski, 1990).

Sources of Learning. Given that the important learnings acquired by overseas student teachers encompass more community and world perspectives and influences than those reported by conventional student teachers, a logical question is, *who* or *what* were the sources of these nontraditional learnings? The respondents were asked to identify the main source for each important learning from a listing of 17 possibilities, including both human and nonhuman, school and nonschool entities. Simplified into source clusters, the possibilities included Community People (host family, parents of pupils, etc.); School Professionals (head teacher, classroom teacher, etc.); School Pupils (in own and other classrooms); Physical Things (geography, museums/historical sites, etc.); and Listening, Reading, and Reflecting (media, host nation authors, the self, etc.).

An interesting trend in these data is that conventional student teachers cite school-related sources (professionals and pupils combined) a total of 83% of the time, whereas overseas participants credit the same sources only 49.5% of the time. Why the difference? Overseas participants have already completed their stateside student teaching experience and probably feel less need to depend as heavily on school professionals and pupils for new information. Many of the skills and techniques they acquired stateside can readily be applied to their overseas classrooms; plus, having successfully completed one experience is likely to give them greater confidence in their own teaching abilities, decision-making skills, and other professional areas. Thus, the school-related people would be perceived as important learning sources when curricular, pedagogical, or procedural variations were encountered as a result of cultural differences.

However, most striking is the difference between overseas and conventional student teachers in their identification of Community People as important sources of learning, with percentages of 34.4% and only 8.9%, respectively. Academic and cultural expectations require that Overseas Project participants live with host families in the local community and meet people outside the school environment, interview them, and join in their activities. To fulfill these requirements, many participants seek out and attend local churches, exercise classes, and meetings of various interest groups and clubs. Further, they generally become integral members of the host family during their overseas experience and depend on the family members for support, companionship, and advice on daily survival. As the relationship develops, information about respective cultures is shared, stereotypes are dissolved, and differences in lifestyles are examined and perhaps adopted. No wonder the overseas student teachers rate their host families and other community people as such significant sources of learning; these individuals become a focal part of the participants' daily experience. Plus, involvement of this nature leads to a better understanding of how citizens in the host community live, what they think, and what they value—vital learnings for educators serving the community's children. Conventional student teachers, however, are less likely to gain these important insights about the community surrounding their school, because such requirements and expectations are generally not included in their field experience assignments (Mahan & Stachowski, 1990, 1993-1994).

Other Findings. Several other important outcomes reported by Overseas Project student teachers have been documented. For example, when the acquisition of knowledge on global issues is made a focus of the international field experience, considerable learning takes place on a large number and wide range of topics, complete with facts, personal insights, and classroom follow-up. Fifty-five Overseas Project participants generated 210 essays on global issues, spanning 56 different topics, such as pollution and environmental destruction, AIDS, terrorism, overpopulation, and the emergence of Japan as an economic world power. The soundness of their classroom applications suggested that most of these novice educators will enter their first teaching positions with new understandings about global education and how it can be an integral part of elementary and secondary classrooms (Mahan & Stachowski, 1992).

In a study designed to examine student teachers' understanding of the cultural and national values, attitudes, and beliefs held by host nation citizens, and the impact of these values on their own actions in the host schools, homes, and communities, 80 project participants generated 240 distinct responses falling into nine categories, such as Environmental Protection/Conservation/ Respect, Importance of Family and Friends, Appreciation of National History and Traditions, and Less Materialism/Wastefulness. Their responses indicated that these future teachers were looking beyond the walls of their classrooms and schools and beyond the parameters of their own backgrounds and often limited experiences to ask: "Why are things this way?" and "How can I be most effective in this environment?" Again, such learnings will enable educators to better understand the diversity that exists in the communities from which their pupils come (Mahan & Stachowski, 1993).

Conclusion

International field experiences are a viable means of broadening the perspectives and expanding the knowledge base of preservice educators. When undergirded by a solid preparatory phase, on-site academic assignments, and evaluation and follow-up, such experiences can result in significant learning about topics, issues, and aspects of human life seldom considered during conventional student teaching assignments. Further, host communities play a vital role in educating the student teachers, as opposed to sole reliance on classroom teachers and university supervisors. Gumbert (1985) gloomily assessed: "Most of the people in the world acquire only a hazy and distorted idea of the lives and aspirations of other people. Responses to other nations too frequently are made up of a mixture of selfishness, innocence, and ignorance; too rarely of genuine concern, knowledge, and understanding" (p. 9).

International field experiences represent one way of reversing this trend, by preparing future teachers not only pedagogically, but also for their role as citizens of a global society—citizens who are knowledgeable about and comfortable with the similarities and differences of all cultures. Educators, who have journeyed beyond the safety net of their own familiar experience to immerse themselves into the unknown, can similarly journey locally and annually into the lives and communities of their culturally diverse pupils; certainly, they will find this journey no less challenging, no less instructional, because it happens here in the United States. The result will likely be the realization that all cultures—indeed, all children—are special; full of beauty, strength, and dreams; possessing unique ways of expressing them.

References

Benjamin, S. (1985). Cultural diversity: What are the implications for teachers? *The Clearing House, 59*(2), 80-82.

Bennett, C. I. (1990). *Comprehensive multicultural education* (2nd ed.). Boston: Allyn & Bacon.

Gumbert, E. B. (1985). Introduction. In E. B. Gumbert (Ed.), *World of strangers: International education in the United States, Russia, Britain, and India* (pp. 3-10). Atlanta, GA: Center for Cross-Cultural Education.

Guyton, E., & McIntyre, D. J. (1990). Student teaching and school experiences. In W. R. Houston (Ed.), *Handbook of research on teacher education* (pp. 514-534). New York: Macmillan.

Hersh, R. H., Hull, R., & Leighton, M. S. (1982). Student teaching. In H. E. Mitzel (Ed.), *The encyclopedia of educational research* (pp. 1812-1822). New York: Free Press.

Korsgaard, R. (1994). *Overseas student teaching.* River Falls, WI: Foundation for International Education.

Lanier, J. E., & Little, J. W. (1986). Research on teacher education. In M. C. Wittrock (Ed.), *Handbook of research on teaching* (pp. 527-569). New York: Macmillan.

Mahan, J. M., & Stachowski, L. L. (1985). Overseas student teaching: A model, important outcomes, recommendations. *International Education, 15*(1), 9-28.

Mahan, J. M., & Stachowski, L. L. (1990). New horizons: Student teaching abroad to enrich understanding of diversity. *Action in Teacher Education, 12*(3), 13-21.

Mahan, J. M., & Stachowski, L. L. (1992). A replicable effort to make learning about global issues an outcome of teacher preparation. *International Education, 22*(1), 5-19.

Mahan, J. M., & Stachowski, L. L. (1993, February). *Impact of cultural and national values, attitudes, and beliefs of foreign citizens upon U.S. student teachers abroad.* Paper presented at the national conference of the Association of Teacher Educators, Los Angeles.

Mahan, J. M., & Stachowski, L. L. (1993-1994). Diverse, previously uncited sources of professional learning reported by student teachers serving in culturally different communities. *National Forum of Teacher Education Journal, 3*(1), 21-28.

Pickert, S. M. (1992). *Preparing for a global community: Achieving an international perspective in higher education* (Report 2—1992 ASHE-ERIC Higher Education Reports). Washington, DC: George Washington University.

Wilson, A. H. (1982). Cross-cultural experiential learning for teachers. *Theory Into Practice, 21*(3), 184-192.

Zimpher, N. A. (1989). The RATE Project: A profile of teacher education students. *Journal of Teacher Education, 40*(6), 27-30.

❖ 10 ❖

Bits and Pieces

Everything Else You Wanted to Know About Field Experiences of the Future

GLORIA APPELT SLICK
KENNETH BURRETT

As we envision the future of field experiences in teacher preparation, it is of utmost importance that we reflect upon the successes of the past. Changes are occurring at astounding rates. Our challenge is to keep pace and, if possible, to surge forward, ready for what is to come. As we travel into the future we can take with us some valuable lessons we have learned about teacher preparation. One of the most important things we have come to know is that effective, practicing professionals rely upon reflective processes to assess their successes and areas of need. They practice their reflectivity continuously. We have also learned how important field experiences are in the preparation of new teachers. There is a current cry for quality field experiences with collaboration between the institutions of higher learning and the public schools. These pleas for more interaction require new roles for all parties involved and new visions of operation and relationships. This chapter explores five major areas of concern for field experiences in teacher education that we feel will have a tremendous impact on the success of future teachers and their ability to meet the challenges of teaching in the 21st century—the age of information and personal excellence in a global community.

Leadership

Beginning with the publication of *A Nation at Risk* (National Commission on Excellence in Education, 1983), educators have sought to address issues surrounding the changes needed to update, assess, and restructure the existing education system. The system was apparently not meeting the needs of the public, the demands of the business community, and the requirements of preparing citizenry for a global community. Proponents of the most recent attempt to restructure the education system, called systemic reform, believe that reform must encompass all aspects of the education system. In the past, most of the educational reforms only focused on remedying one component of the system, that is, curriculum. Systemic reform, on the other hand, takes into consideration the interrelatedness of all components that function together in the education system. It realizes that as one component changes, so must the others in order to maintain the integrity, continuity, and consistency of the entire system. To accomplish this goal, all players in the system must be considered as viable, potential, and ongoing contributors to the change and function of the system. Systemic reform is viewed as a shift from a more traditional education system to one that emphasizes interconnectedness, active learning, shared decision making, and high levels of achievement for all students (Anderson, 1993, p. 14). If systemic reform is to not only take place but also continue as an ongoing evolutionary process that will allow the system to grow and change, then the practice of shared decision making and consensus building must begin immediately. This relatively new governance process necessitates the incorporation of insightful site-based management. If this is the direction in which our profession is going, then the question becomes, are we preparing our undergraduates, the teachers of the future, to adequately function in a system that requires them to assume leadership responsibilities in a site-based management system? Furthermore, what are we doing for our preservice teachers in field experiences to prepare them for the leadership roles they will be expected to handle?

Traditionally, leadership has been consistently characterized by the central values of power and control (Patterson, 1993, p. 2). Organizations have been conceived, constructed, and evaluated on the premise that leaders are responsible for directing and controlling the organization (Patterson, 1993, p. 2). This type of "boss" leading, which is top-down, is not the perception of what is needed for systemic change. Management alone, although a component of leadership, does not fulfill the requirements of systemic change or site-based management. Management is the act of coordinating people and resources to efficiently produce goods or services in an organization (Patterson, 1993, p. 2). The kind of leader that is needed for site-based management, which involves all the players at the site, is one who encourages participation, shares power and information, and enhances the self-worth of others and their part in the whole scheme of the system. In the organization of tomorrow, leading is defined as the process of influencing others to achieve mutually agreed-upon purposes for the organization. This type of leadership is called transformational leadership. It involves motivating others for the good of the organization by transforming their self-interest into the goals of the organization. This is unlike the old transactional leadership, which operated on the basis of doling out rewards for good work and punishment for bad (Billard, 1992, p. 69). Transformational leadership is often referred to as a participatory style of leadership. Are our new teachers ready to participate?

Typically, teacher education programs focus on refining content specialties and instructional strategies. There appears to be little inclusion of leadership development in most teacher preparation programs. The following are suggestions for ways to prepare our preservice teachers to become participants in site-based management and capable of responding to a transformational leader. First, in our undergraduate education and methods classes, professors could practice participatory leadership in the way they teach their classes. The content material as well as the strategies used for presenting it could foster the skills needed for participatory leadership. The skills of decision making could be incorporated into group collaborative projects. Consensus building could be experienced through the resolution of debatable issues surrounding the content being presented. Second, methods classes can present simulations of problem solving concerning issues that teachers will face in the school setting. Aided by technology, whether through compressed video of on-site classroom situations, or through interaction with CD programs, preservice teachers can be propelled into the "real" arena of everyday problem solving in the public school classroom. Such programs can also realistically create faculty group meetings that are centered on collaborative endeavors requiring decision making and/or consensus building.

Third, there should be many ways that preservice teachers can engage in leadership activities during field experiences that would prepare them to be successful, site-based management participants when they become a part of a public school faculty. It is important that reflection be a part of each of the activities listed below.

1. Have students shadow a principal and observe the many interactions and responsibilities with which that person deals.
2. Sit in on faculty group meetings in which participatory leadership is being employed.
3. Participate in decision-making meetings with faculty concerning curriculum decisions, disciplinary action, policy changes, scheduling decisions.
4. Plan and conduct a meeting of peers, utilizing leadership skills that promote participatory decision making by the group.

5. Tape a faculty meeting and then critique it for the effective use of the transformational leadership style.

6. Have the preservice teacher videotape some of his or her lessons being taught, then analyze them for the leadership style that the preservice teacher is using while teaching.

7. Have preservice teachers interview administrators—principals, supervisors, and superintendents—regarding their perceptions of their own leadership style. Subsequently, have the preservice teacher attend board meetings or other meetings where these leaders are engaged in leadership situations.

8. Attend and/or view via videotape central office administrative meetings. Critique for leadership style employed during those meetings.

Ultimately, in order to be fully prepared as a new teacher, the preservice teacher must undergo a variety of leadership training experiences. This will provide preparation for successfully contributing to the site-based management procedures a principal employs at his or her campus. Finally, preservice teachers can learn about effective leadership through *observing positive role models* of leadership, both in the college classrooms and in the public schools. *Opportunities to engage in leadership experiences* should also be available to them in the college classroom and in the public school setting. By learning and then applying effective leadership skills in their own classrooms, preservice teachers will, in turn, be models of leadership for the students they will be teaching.

A prime opportunity for employing transformational leadership would be in the field experience program. With so many different publics being served by field experience offices, it seems appropriate that the leadership style of the director would be participatory. Consequently, the field director has a prime opportunity to model for preservice teachers, as well as university faculty and public school personnel, the transformational leadership style. To facilitate this type of leadership, the director should establish advisory and decision-making committees whose responsibility it is to give advice concerning the programs and functions of the field experience office. As a result of this type of participation in the operation of the programs offered, there is a team effort and spirit that makes it possible for everyone to work together to achieve a common goal. This is the ideal. The people on these committees must represent all persons and systems affected by the field experience programs. Therefore, there are representative preservice teachers, classroom teachers who serve as professional models, university faculty, public school administrators, and, whenever possible, pupils from the public school classrooms. Preservice teachers should have the opportunity to observe and react to some of the decision-making committee meetings that occur and involve the various publics. This will give them an example of how participatory management is orchestrated by a transformational leader.

Another possibility for demonstrating the transformational leadership style to professional cohorts as well as preservice teachers occurs in the operational management of the field experience office itself. Secretaries, clerks, assistant directors, and all the university supervisors/professors engaged in operating the field experience office should have their say about how it is operated. Each person feels that his or her opinion and ideas have been considered and incorporated when they are appropriate in terms of the overall program goals.

When visitors come into the field experience office, they should see a well-coordinated group of people functioning in concert with one another. The office staff know and exhibit in their behavior what the common cause is and consistently work toward achieving that established cause. The resultant effect is a smooth-running office with satisfied personnel in charge. There is an air of respect and appreciation for all who play a part. Students' concerns and needs are seen as a priority and are handled professionally. Because the transformational leader values everyone in the organization, this attitude becomes the operational style of all the other team members.

Partnerships

What are the needs of schools as we approach the 21st century? What are the implications for teachers? How can we prepare teachers to meet the educational mandates of today and tomorrow? The best of theory and practice dictates a paradigm shift in the structure and substance of teacher education. This mandate applies to field-based programs. Change is the result of program initiatives from dedicated professionals. A collaborative structure that joins the scholarship of college and university, the excellence in practice of school personnel, and the resources of corporate and community organizations can forge an effective mechanism for promoting professional excellence.

Cooperation between schools and teacher education programs exists in the placement of pre-student teachers and student teachers, and the conduct of some in-service programs. Influential national reports recommend formalizing and expanding these connections to establish collaboration and partnership arrangements between schools and teacher education units. Of late there is support for the idea that schools include community agencies and corporate resources as partners. It can also be argued that these resources can be connected with teacher education efforts. It makes sense that those sharing a common vision of excellence work together.

Also, national organizations list the ability to foster relationships as a required competency for beginning teachers. "The teacher fosters relationships with school colleagues, parents, and agencies in the larger community to support students' learning and well being"(Interstate New Teacher and Support Consortium, 1992). It would seem that teacher education programs could structure partnerships as a means of providing appropriate clinical sites for developing this competency in new teachers.

Collaboration can generate many benefits. Specific profiles are related to the form of any particular agreement. Some general and common benefits are:

- Focusing university research and scholarship on current school problems

- Connecting university preparation practices with the world of practice
- Joint ventures in evaluation, planning, and in-service programs
- Mutual staff development opportunities
- Interdisciplinary perspectives on problem solving
- Access to a much larger talent pool from the community agency and corporate partners
- Access to the resources of a much broader community
- Strengthened position for securing external funds, including grants
- Increased efficiency in using resources
- Occasions for teachers and teacher educators to assume new roles and exercise leadership
- Access to community concerns over education and teacher education
- Input from experienced professionals for improving teacher education programs
- Impact on school programs at the point of delivery
- Expanded opportunities for action research and publication
- A mechanism for reflecting societal priorities into school and preparation programs
- The environment supportive of translating theory into practice

Pursuit of these benefits can result in the establishment of some creative and innovative structures. These might include:

- Professional development schools
- Corporate/university/school collaboratives
- Interdisciplinary training and teaching teams
- Expansive school volunteer programs
- Classroom teaching teams, including members from university, community, and corporate sectors

- Community-oriented communication programs
- Schools and school programs sponsored by corporate and foundation funding
- Regional teacher education and in-service collabotatives

These innovative structures are supported by:

- Mentors, who stimulate career development activities, serve as confidants, provide practical advice, and establish supportive relationships
- Volunteers, from corporations and agencies, who tutor, conduct problem-solving sessions, contribute professional expertise, and share techniques and knowledge from a range of professions
- Initiators of special projects, who focus possibilities for special community connections
- Corporate and agency trainers, who share their specific core of professional knowledge and skills
- Advisors for curriculum, who emphasize cutting-edge developments from private and public sectors

Through collaboration and partnership relationships, it is possible to:

1. Connect community resources with the education and teacher education process.
2. Infuse programs with a realistic awareness of the community, and emphasize the outcomes of schooling and responsibilities of teachers.
3. Supplement teacher education programs with relevant learning experiences.
4. Establish excellence in teaching as a community responsibility.

Unlike improvement proposed in earlier decades, reform and quality improvement now seem possible only through collaborative efforts of teachers, teacher educators, parents, administrators, and community members, along with the assistance of community agencies and the corporate sector. This happens only when all are connected to a shared vision of school quality. The mandate is clearly to build collaborative relationships internally and externally.

Diversified Classrooms

When new teachers walk into their classrooms today, they are entering classrooms quite different from those of 20 years ago. The teachers of tomorrow will have, on the average, two to three different cultures represented in their classrooms. There might not be a definitive majority, but if there is, it might not be the Anglo culture of the past. If not fully prepared to teach in the multicultural classroom, the teacher might make some egregious assumptions that could be damaging to the students they teach. Diversity abounds in today's classrooms. The children represent a variety of cultures, abilities, attitudes, and beliefs, all of which have a tremendous impact on the teaching responsibilities of the classroom teacher. It is difficult for a new teacher to understand and cope with all the various cultures and capabilities of children within the contemporary classroom. Beginning teachers are generally consumed with learning how to manage the job of teaching, let alone the complexities of dealing with diversity in the classroom. In the best of circumstances this is a difficult job. Teacher educators must respond to the critical issues posed by demographic changes in the population of future classrooms. Inclusion of children with special needs into the regular classroom poses still another variable that the preservice teacher must experience in order to be prepared to address those children's needs. This inclusion of children within the regular classroom further compounds the diversity that new teachers will face in the classrooms of the future. Field experiences that provide preservice teachers with opportunities to observe and work with master teachers, who model ways to manage and teach children in the inclusion classroom, are a must. Programs need to provide preservice teachers with many opportunities to work with children of varying disabilities and capabilities. In essence, because of the inclusion movement, all student teachers become special education student teachers. With so much potential diversity in classrooms of today and tomorrow, preservice teachers will need skills, teaching strategies, and a knowledge base that prepare them to model and exemplify someone who appreciates the diversity that exists in classrooms. Field experience programs that provide an articulated program of immersion experiences will go a long way toward facilitating such preparation.

There are some guiding principles that new teachers should be taught in order to prepare them to ably manage and teach in the diverse classroom. It is the teacher's responsibility to model being a global citizen. In order to do this teachers must be comfortable with providing:

1. A positive learning environment evidenced in the physical environment as well as the emotional environment in the class;
2. A positive attitude toward diversity;
3. An ability to model respect, appreciation, and understanding for all children and the varying cultures, belief systems, and capabilities they represent; and
4. A positive belief in the worth of all children.

The diverse classrooms will be characterized by children bearing different languages, cultures, cognitive needs, and special learning needs. Teacher preparation programs need to involve preservice teachers in these diverse environments early in their preparation. This immersion may well occur in the classrooms these children occupy. Or, another way to aid future teachers in becoming familiar with other cultures and belief systems is to immerse them in the culture through community involvement/ service programs. Through university/community cooperative efforts, teacher education students can participate in numerous community service projects that will allow them some insight into a culture's value system and customs. Through careful guidance by the university faculty, students will, through reflective practices, begin coming to terms with not only their own belief systems but also the issue of whether they can respect those of others. Teachers who cannot come to terms with appreciating, respecting, and understanding, as closely as possible, the cultures and characteristics of the children they teach should carefully consider whether they belong in the classroom. Why? Because, today and in the future, more than ever the classroom teacher will be the principal model of a global citizen for the children in that classroom.

When the time arrives to determine a preservice teacher's field experiences, it will be to the student's advantage to provide experiences that are representative of both urban and rural environments. To have a comprehensive view of the profession's challenges, each student should experience the diversity that exists within the profession. To consider oneself certifiable in the profession, one should have as many experiences with the varying cultural and disability aspects of the profession as possible. Consequently, of necessity, the student would be placed in a variety of diverse environments for practicum experiences.

Academic experiences can support the field experiences in developing cultural sensitivity. For instance, teacher education programs should provide foreign language instruction as a requisite in their instructional programs. It is well known that a culture's language is a window into the life of that culture. Such programs as those provided by *Command Languages*, special multilingual menus of languages and cultural instruction, are ideal for the multicultural environment in which new teachers will find themselves. The *Command Languages* programs provide teachers with the ability to function at a general conversation level in numerous languages—Spanish, Japanese, German, French, Italian, and Russian (Slick, 1993). Along with the language instruction, students learn about cultural information that is shared by native speakers. The programs open windows to the world and bring life to the people of other countries through their language and culture. Such language and cultural instruction should be a part of a teacher's training so that he or she will be prepared to comprehend and function in a classroom representative of diverse cultures, diverse abilities, and diverse learning styles.

Beyond the preservice teacher's knowledge of languages and cultural values and beliefs, there are some absolutes that must exist in the diversified classrooms of the future. Within the diversified classroom there must exist for all children:

1. A sense of belonging
2. A sense of identity
3. A sense of purpose
4. A sense of security
5. A sense of fairness and respect
6. A sense of appreciation for the value of each individual
7. A sense of competence
8. A sense of accomplishment

As teachers and students learn to cope with the multicultural, diverse environment in which they will exist, both in and out of the classroom, all of them will grapple with who they are and what their place is in the whole scheme of things. Such fundamental questions about one's existence can be both frightening and challenging. Together, in mutual appreciation and respect, we can build positive, worthwhile individuals who will create an exciting new world full of beautiful diversity.

Author, artist, teacher, mother, grandmother, and Texas Hall of Famer Rosa Guerrero has a lovely way of expressing the beauty that comes from diversity: "We are the threads that are woven into a multicultural tapestry, the fabric of American life. We are like notes in a chord of music . . . if all the notes were the same, there would be no harmony, no real beauty . . . because harmony is based on differences, not similarities" (Guerrero, 1993, p. 2). She states further: "Our country is a multicultural tapestry, a mosaic of many people. Each group that represents our land is unique and different. Because of our differentness, we can all contribute something important to the fabric of the American life. Therefore, each person is special and unequalled" (p. 19).

The biggest challenge rests in the hands of the adults who influence children, the parents and the teachers. Children do not come into the world with hatred and prejudice. They learn these from adults. It is true that there are many campaigns to combine the efforts of the community and the school to improve the learning environment and opportunities for children. One of the biggest challenges will be for adults to overcome their prejudice and hatred in order to teach children how to live together in harmony. Teachers can and do have a tremendous impact in such endeavors.

International Education

If it can be argued that a primary goal of schooling is to prepare students to live in a world community, then as a corollary it is appropriate to educate teachers to support that goal. Study abroad programs are a common option on American campuses. It is not unusual for teacher education programs to offer a student teaching abroad program. These programs are an important educational experience in broadening the education of future teachers. Student teaching abroad provides an immersion experience in another culture, a counterpoint from which to view American culture and educational practice, experiences in new paradigms of school organization and methodology, sensitivity to the demands and opportunities of global citizenship, and a direct curriculum experience in global education.

The development of student teaching abroad programs expands the traditional context of teacher education and results in the creation of a substantively different curriculum. It can be argued that international experiences are not a nice supplement to a program; they are a necessary condition. Though the mandate is clear, implementation is not easy. On a conceptual level:

- Develop goals and objectives in relation to the interdisciplinary nature of the experience.
- Focus on teacher development.
- Develop a clear vision of the school in the changing world of the 21st century.

- Conceive of the relationships with host universities and schools as partnerships.
- Relate the student teaching abroad experience to the curriculum of your teacher education unit.

On a planning level:

- Invite the support of the dean, provost, and president of your institution.
- Establish an advisory council of interested faculty from education from across the university, and from community and corporate constituencies. Alumni are also a valuable resource.
- Develop a vision statement, relating overseas student teaching to general education purposes and to the teacher education curriculum.
- Petition the teacher education curriculum committee for acceptance and approval.
- Elicit endorsements from community sources.
- Approach your advisory council as a source of contacts and potential grant support.
- Identify potential host institutions or overseas schools. (Suggestions are often available through special interest groups of national teacher education groups, such as the ATE. Regional accrediting agencies are also good source for listings of accredited schools.)
- Initiate introductory correspondence. Inquire about interest, comprehensivness of support services, willingness and capability to support the curriculum of your institution, and possibilities for partnership agreements.
- Give priority to those who indicate an interest in programmatic reciprocity. Certainly this includes an expressed interest to support your curriculum. It may also include willingness to negotiate faculty and student exchanges, sponsored seminars for practicing teachers, arrangements

to host regional conferences, and, certainly, connections via E-mail and distance learning.

- Select the colleges and universities of choice.
- Develop written materials that describe your institution, teacher education unit, and specific goals and objectives for the student teaching abroad program.
- Seek the endorsement and support from central administration to schedule on-site negotiations at the overseas programs of your choice.
- Develop your financial position.

On the negotiation level:

- Schedule your visits. Fax and E-mail are very useful.
- Ensure that your materials are part of the meeting agenda.
- Establish a partnership orientation.
- Discuss a time line for programs. Consider staged implementation.
- Establish program parameters.
- Openly and honestly discuss financial arrangements.
- Attempt to establish payment amounts in the currency of the paying country. Adjust costs with exchange rates. Currency fluctuations will affect budgets. Financial arrangements are best negotiated on a yearly basis.
- Follow conversations with letters of understanding.
- Confirm arrangements with specific letters of agreement.

On the implementation level:

- Specify the program in detail, with each party signing the agreement.
- Include intensive preparation for all participants, including students, supervisors, and faculty.
- Include consideration of culture, language phrases, telephoning skills, menus, and transportation.

- Provide resource materials for parents, spouses, and significant others not traveling.
- Provide specific policy manuals and program materials for students and supervisors traveling overseas.
- Develop a contract for those traveling, clearly spelling out conditions of participation and procedures for cancelling the placement. Do not be shy in stating expectations.
- Ensure that the experience is documented. Require portfolios. Collect pictures, diaries, videotapes, and whatever else can be obtained.
- Establish regular communication with your contact person.
- Build in time for students to enjoy the experience.
- Visit the site, especially during the early cycles.
- Invite your students to conduct seminars on their return, to share experiences and publicize the opportunity.
- Post a display to highlight the accomplishments.

Build a program, not a travel agency. Remain true to your vision. Enjoy the experience. Build cooperative partnerships. Take pride and joy from the excitement and opportunities you have opened to members of your academic community.

Technology

Technology should, and will, have an impact on field experiences of the future. Technological advances can catapult the university classroom of the future closer to the public school classrooms throughout teacher preparation programs. CD classroom simulations that require student interaction and responses will provide early opportunities for teacher education students to make choices about appropriate responses to pupils and classroom situations. Expert opinions that are included on the CD programs will give immediate feedback to students as to the accuracy of their problem-solving choices.

Compressed video linkages will provide on-site, instantaneous opportunities for observation and interactive dialogue among linked parties. Interactive distance learning will link sites, allowing students in one part of the country to view the educational settings and transactions of another. With modems and Internet connections, international dialogue among educators will be at their fingertips. The Internet will bring collegial dialogue to a new plateau, not only with counterpart teachers and educators but also with student teachers participating in study abroad programs during their field experience assignments. These windows of information and experience will provide a plethora of examples of classroom and professional ideology for reflection.

Within the confines of the university's territory, E-mail can provide a potential ongoing, interactive network among university supervisors and their students in the field. Interaction with university supervisors would not be limited to a few on-site visits. Logging in on a daily, or at least once a week, basis will allow supervisors and students to keep close contact and afford cooperative groups numerous opportunities to reflect together on progress.

PC accessibility to students as well as university supervisors and cooperating teachers will indeed provide numerous means for healthy interaction among all three parties. Some of the options that technology can bring teacher preparation programs have been briefly discussed herein. The following suggest still other avenues for use:

1. Multimedia packages for instructional modeling in the college classroom
2. PC applications that assist students and teachers in record-keeping and instructional planning
3. Accessing of reference catalogs for research
4. Downloading staff development programs from around the country
5. Videotaping of students' teaching; playback transmission on compressed video for supervisor's critique

6. Dissemination of content material through interactive distance learning programs
7. Live viewing of the instructional process in the public schools
8. Professional networking for student teachers and mentor teachers
9. Professional networking with professional organizations and their members
10. In-service training for professors that are appropriate for adult learners

Full utilization of the technological advances available to us requires training and experiences that allow professors to become familiar with the options available to them. We must have hands-on opportunities to test the numerous ways that the technology available to us can benefit our instructional endeavors. In order to appeal to their intellect and self-respect, university faculty members must be allowed to discover possibilities and make choices of involvement with the new means of instruction made possible with technology. They must be convinced of the need to change before they can be models of change. If the teachers we train are to truly become users of the technology available to them, they must view us modeling its use in the classes we teach.

With the information superhighway in place and satellite transmissions making the world accessible at almost any time of day or night, the sky may not be the limit anymore. Perhaps, not even the universe is the limit. Suffice it to say that technology is the key to the world of tomorrow. The windows that are being opened are overwhelming, exciting, challenging, and limited only by our imagination. Technology can connect the classroom to the world, redefining the architecture of the school and blurring the distinction between the university classroom and the field. Technology will truly launch us into a global society; therefore, we must prepare ourselves for teaching the future citizens of the world.

References

Anderson, B. (1993). The stages of systemic change. *Educational Leadership, 51*(1), 68-73.

Billard, M. (1992, March). Do women make better managers? *Working Woman*, pp. 68-73.

Guerrero, R. (1993). *Rosa*. El Paso, TX: PDX Press.

Interstate New Teacher Assessment and Support Consortium. (1992). *CCSSO draft standards for licensing beginning teachers* (No. 10), 10-30.

Patterson, J. L. (1993). *Leadership for tomorrow's schools*. Alexandria, VA: Association for Supervision and Curriculum Development.

Slick, S. L. (1993). *World languages for business professionals*. Petal, MS: Command Languages.

Index

CORWIN
PRESS

The Corwin Press Logo—a raven striding across an open book—
represents the happy union of courage and learning. We are a
professional-level publisher of books and journals for K-12 educators, and we are committed to creating and providing resources that
embody these qualities. Corwin's motto is "Success for All Learners."